Why Not Be a Mystic?

Why Not Be a Mystic?

Frank X. Tuoti

CROSSROAD · NEW YORK

The author expresses his gratitude to The Merton Legacy Trust
for permission to quote extensively from Thomas Merton's manuscript
"The Inner Experience."

1995

The Crossroad Publishing Company
370 Lexington Avenue, New York, NY 10017

Printed in the United States of America

Library of Congress Cataloging-in-Publication Data

Tuoti, Frank X.
    Why not be a mystic / Frank X. Tuoti.
        p.   cm.
    Includes bibliographical references.
    ISBN 0-8245-1503-X; 0-8245-1453-X (pbk.)
    1. Mysticism.   I. Title.
    BV5082.2.T86 1995
    248.2'2—dc20   94-29704
                                            CIP

*This book is gratefully dedicated
to those who have changed my life:*

*Thomas Merton, once brother Trappist and mentor,
George Maloney, friend and staretz,
my wife, Gale, my earth,
and to the woman Juan Diego loved.*

The only cure for the angst of modern man is mysticism.

— *Thomas Merton*

Contents

❧

Acknowledgments

෴

I express my profound gratitude and appreciation to long-time friend George A. Maloney, S.J., without whose encouragement this book would not have gotten past the first few chapters. He graciously not only undertook to lend his distinguished name to this effort, but also acted as general editor and consulting theologian. With Merton, George Maloney led me to the study of the Eastern and Oriental Church and Desert Fathers, who laid the foundation stones of Christian mysticism for all ages to come.

Heartfelt appreciation is extended to Lucy Peerenboom, a devoted wife and mother, spiritual companion in the Lord on the contemplative journey. Lucy patiently read each chapter several times as they were being written and revised, always finding ways to improve them. There is hardly a chapter that has not benefited from Lucy's insightful comments and suggestions.

Introduction

by George A. Maloney, S.J.

❦

Mysticism is a phenomenon that has rapidly swept through the world during the second half of the twentieth century and will surely continue to increase as we enter into the third millennium. Mysticism takes many forms, which should convince us of a basic hunger in all human beings for an intimate union with the Divine. In all human beings there exists a propensity toward mysticism. We have within ourselves an inner drive toward union with the Supreme Reality. If we call that Reality God, we are saying that all finite beings must ultimately fail to satisfy that thirst in all of us for deeper, more intense interpenetration with God.

For most of us it takes several decades of our lives of futile searching to realize that nothing in the world can ever satisfy us but God. For it is God who has given us this basic drive to possess him and be possessed, to possess the Unpossessable, which — in the words of the poet Francis Thompson — makes all other possessions vain.

God is love (1 Jn 4:8). God's loving presence as personalized relations of uncreated energies of love surrounds us, permeates us, bathes us constantly in his great loving communication of himself as a self-giving Love to us. This is an ongoing self-giving on the part of God the Father through his Son in his Spirit. Or should we not better say it is more an ongoing discovery on our part how completely this self-giving God is always toward us and how intimately close God is to us?

Father William McNamara, O.C.D., describes such a consistent contemplative attitude of discovering God in his inner presence found in ourselves and in all other creatures:

> Contemplation is a pure intuition of being born of love. It is experiential awareness of reality and a way of entering into immediate communion with reality. Reality? Why, that means people, trees, lakes, mountains. You can study things, but unless you enter into this intuitive communion with them, you can only know about them, you don't know them. To take a long, loving look at something...a child, a glass of wine, a beautiful meal ...this is a natural act of contemplation of loving admiration.... To be able to do that, there's the rub. All the way through school we are taught to abstract, we are not taught loving awareness.

Contemplation is basically a look toward God in faith, hope, and love. It is standing, as it were, outside of our habitual idea that we have had of ourselves and of God and of others and of the whole world. It is getting down below that false everyday ego and getting into our deepest source where we stand before God, consciously turning toward our Source, our Origin.

We are not dealing here with an exercise of piety alone. We are certainly not dealing with anything that is dependent upon perseverance in a certain method, a way of breathing or sitting. Contemplation is applicable to every human being and, therefore, should be as natural as a baby looking on its father's or mother's face.

Why Not Be a Mystic?

I have been asked by Frank Tuoti, my friend of over twenty years, to write an introduction to his book *Why Not Be a Mystic?* The author entered the Cistercian monastery of

Gethsemani, Kentucky, in 1951 where he came under the influence of brother Trappist Thomas Merton. After a few years he reluctantly had to leave Gethsemani, later embarking upon a successful career in television management in New York and Arizona. He now resides in the Sonoran desert on the outskirts of Tucson with his artist-wife, Gale. Over the past ten years he has been active in teaching Christian audiences about contemplative prayer and the disciplines necessary to grow into deeper prayer.

Here is a voice of a layman, well-gifted to teach those in the world who are not living a strictly so-called monastic life about the universal call of God to all of us to experience deeper union with the indwelling Trinity. He writes in the idiom of everyday people living in today's world to help us understand the treasures found in Holy Scripture and the great mystical teachers of the Church, especially the early Desert Fathers and Mothers, the Church Fathers, the medieval mystical writers like St. John of the Cross, Meister Eckhart, and St. Teresa of Avila, and modern writers like Thomas Merton, his mentor, Thomas Keating, O.C.S.O., Bede Griffiths, O.S.B., and many others.

Immersed in such solid teachings, the author covers very well in thirty-four short chapters the intricacies of the paths of the contemplative life. His own personal, disciplined prayer life shines through as he presents the traditional ancient Fathers' teaching on the mystical life in a manner that people living in today's world can not only understand, but can be strongly challenged to progress in their own thirst for greater union with God and neighbor.

Frank Tuoti summarizes true contemplation as complete surrender at all times to God's energizing love that directs all of us at every step of our lives. He highlights that this is an ongoing process that knows no end. But this evolves into a transforming union with God in a loving oneness between oneself and neighbor and all of God's creatures through purification of self-centeredness in order to enter into transformation in Christ.

This is to live seriously our baptism into the Trinitarian life in which God, Father, Son, and Holy Spirit, become at each moment our complete ALL. Hugh of St. Victor has well described this state of union with God and the world:

> Yes, it is truly the Beloved who visits thee. But he comes invisible, hidden, incomprehensible. He comes to touch thee, not to be seen; to intimate his presence to thee, not to be understood; to make thee taste of him, not to pour himself out in his entirety; to draw thy affection, not to satisfy thy desire; to bestow the first-fruits of his love, not to communicate it in its fullness.
>
> Behold in this the most certain pledge of thy future marriage: that thou art destined to see him and to possess him eternally, because he already gives himself to thee to taste; with what sweetness thou knowest. Therefore, in the times of his absence thou shalt console thyself; and during his visits thou shalt renew thy courage.

Part One

A Treasure Lost: Recovering the Pearl of Great Price

1

Mysticism as Ordinary

❧

The "coming age" about which Karl Rahner wrote well over a decade ago has already descended upon us, and as we approach a new century it will come cascading down wave after great wave. Many understand that we have entered a new evolutionary stage of consciousness, that we are on the cusp of a new age of enlightenment, of understanding ourselves, the cosmos, and the interdependent relationship of all matter and being. In this new age we must begin to "see" as God "sees" — *inwardly*. We must perceive — *through a graced experience of the heart* — the reality of things, most of all the inner truth of every person.

> We are not capable of union with one another on the deepest level until the inner self in each one of us is sufficiently awakened to confront the inner self of the other.
> — *Thomas Merton*[1]

In other words, *we must become mystics!* The sole intent of this book is to make the case that the gift of a contemplative spirituality and the mystical life is open to all who would seek and desire it — a desire motivated not by self-serving interests (for our "self-improvement" or to be able one day to think of ourselves as "mystics," God forbid!) but a response to the first precept to love God with our entire being and others as ourselves.

19

> To be a Christian is to be committed to a largely mystical
> life, . . . to live within the dimensions of a completely mystical
> revelation and communication of the divine being.
>   — *Thomas Merton*[2]

This book is for those who may not perceive the grandeur
of their Christian calling and the possibilities for joy, happiness, and full life that God offers in the profound intimacy
and union of contemplative spirituality. It is for those who
are already "pray-ers" but who have an unexplainable
hunger for something deeper and more experiential. It is for
those who desire to "taste and see that the Lord is sweet" —
not by intellection, but by an ineffable experience of God as
the living core-center of their being. To experience God in this
way, we must go beyond the juiceless formulas of dogma and
doctrine and existentially encounter the Spirit who enkindles
them and makes them a luminous and vivifying reality.

Sadly, the perception exists among the great majority of
Christians, including clergy and religious, that contemplation
and the mystical life are reserved for "predestined saints"
or for those rare few who live as cloistered monks or nuns,
like Trappists or Carthusian hermits. This stands in square
opposition to the teaching and tradition of the Church:

> We must earnestly draw the attention of souls to the condi-
> tions required for the progress of the grace of the virtues and
> the gifts of the Holy Spirit — *the perfect development of
> which is found in the mystical life.*
>   — *Benedict XV*[3]

Fortunately, this error is being gradually corrected by
the teachings of spiritual masters of our time: George Mal-
oney, S.J., Thomas Keating, O.C.S.O., William Johnson, S.J.,
Henri Nouwen, Bede Griffiths, O.S.B. Cam (d. 1993), Basil
Pennington, O.C.S.O., David Steindl-Rast, O.S.B., Yves
Raguin, S.J., Aelred Graham, O.S.B. (d. 1983), Anthony de
Mello, S.J. (d. 1993), John Main, O.S.B. (d. 1984), among

others. Not the least of these was Thomas Merton, whose
influence on the spirituality of the twentieth century has been
singularly profound:

> Why do we think of infused contemplation, mystical prayer,
> as something essentially strange and esoteric, reserved for
> a small class of almost unnatural beings and prohibited to
> everyone else? Infused contemplation is a powerful means of
> sanctification and is intimately connected with the pure and
> perfect love of God which is God's greatest gift to the soul.
> Therefore, if anyone should ask: "Who may desire this gift
> and pray for it?" — the answer is obvious: everybody.
> — *Thomas Merton*[4]

We are all mystics at our core, since God's own seed is
within us (1 Jn 3:9). Indeed, it is this very seed that holds
us lovingly in being. Inasmuch as God has willed to plant his
own seed in us, is it not also his will and desire that this seed
should germinate and extend its leaves and branches like the
mustard tree? The contemplative/mystical life is the flowering
and blossoming of this divine seed. The gift of contemplation
is the experiential discovery that "God has sent the Spirit of
his Son into our hearts" (Gal 4:6), that "in him we live and
breathe and have our being" (Acts 17:28), and though our
physical body is falling daily into decay, we experience "the
inner person being renewed day by day" (2 Cor 4:6).

For the person with little or no spirituality, any talk of
the mystical life will be viewed as fantasy, illuminism, subjec-
tivism, a pathological or psychological "quirk," or, at best,
a subterfuge. We live in an age that touts an intellectual
fashion termed "deconstructive postmodernism," a philosophy that claims not only that mysticism is not universal, but
that it is a cultural construct or artifact, conceived out of
the different cultural/historical backgrounds of a people or
region, and therefore a contrivance. The contemplative instantly penetrates the absurdity of such a proposal by virtue
of an ineffable yet nonetheless authentic experience. Because

it is ineffable, there is no way to adequately express or communicate the experience except to "point" to it or "get close" to it by use of analogy, metaphor, poetry, and the like.

For the Christian, this reality is the crown of the Christian calling on earth, the "breaking open" of God's seed within us and the flowering of this seed into a "mustard tree" in which the birds of the air (the apostolic endeavors of the Church) come and take shelter and nourishment. It is Life becoming aware of itself in a human dilation of profound awe, praise, and gratitude, grounded in Love. It is the Christian becoming fully awake and alive. In Merton's words, it is God discovering himself in us.

> The Christian contemplative seeks the fullest and most living participation in the experience which has come down from those who walked with Christ on earth, who knew Him and saw Him as risen and received from Him the gifts of the Spirit. Christian mystical knowledge of God is not only the dark and apophatic knowledge of Him as hidden and unknown but is, above and beyond that, the experience of the supernatural light of revelation given to all believers in order that it may be developed under the guidance of the Holy Spirit by the gifts of mystical wisdom and knowledge.
> — *Thomas Merton*[5]

Evelyn Underhill, the Anglican mystic of the early part of our century, rightly observed: "It has always been the mystics who have revitalized the Church. Mysticism will flourish *when enough people desire it*" (emphasis added). We might add that wherever there is enlightened spiritual direction, solid teaching, and sound books on the mystical life, contemplatives will abound. Nothing could be more salutary for the Church than to be bulging with mystics!

This book attempts to make the point, as the great mystical theologians teach, that the mystical/contemplative life is nothing more and nothing less than the *ordinary Christian life* in full flowering, the normal development of "common" sanctifying grace received at baptism, which does not require extraordinary graces. *The living Trinity within us is extraordinary grace enough!*

Though in our own age it need not be so — and will not be so in some future age — the lived experience of the mystical life is "a road less traveled." The decision to commit ourselves to the spiritual journey cannot be likened, except outwardly, to the decision to pursue an "interest" such as philosophy, astronomy, science, the arts, or, for that matter, basketball. Such a decision is a response to a silent, secret, deeply inward call to set out on a lifelong and arduous journey of interior transformation in search of God, to one day "find" God and "see" God in an obscure yet most real experiential interior vision. Once the call is heard, in Thomas Keating's words, you've got to go, no matter the cost.

Karl Rahner, sometimes called the Mystical Doctor of the twentieth century, similarly teaches that "mysticism occurs within the framework of normal graces," remarking that those who teach that mystical experience does not require extraordinary graces "are certainly right." "Mysticism, Rahner writes, "is not confined to a privileged few."[6] I know of no eminent theologian or spiritual master of our time who does not subscribe to this teaching and who does not insist on the universal call to contemplation and the mystical life.

As we plead our case and take the reader through certain aspects of the contemplative/mystical experience, we have drawn on the *lived tradition* of the Church, Catholic and Orthodox, citing the Church Fathers, the saints, Doctors of the Church, great mystical theologians, and the testimony of modern masters of the spiritual life. All genuine Christian mysticism must be grounded in sound theology lest it run the real risk of being a self-styled kind of counterfeit mysticism. Conversely, there can be no true theology without the experiential ingredient of mysticism. In drawing on the masters of the spiritual life, we have avoided using technical and theological terms, except in those instances where it seemed more clarifying to do so.

The reader should not look upon this effort as a course in "Contemplation 101"! — as if the mystical life could be taught or objectified or dissected under some kind of "spiritual microscope." It is my hope that these pages will lead the reader to the investigation of other more substantive books on this subject, including many that have richly fed and nourished me. To that end, a substantial, albeit incomplete, bibliography has been included.

I make no claim to originality, striving only to recast in existential and contemporary language what has been handed down, lived, and treasured since the earliest Christian centuries. I have attempted to be sensitive to the desirability of inclusive language except where to do so seemed forced or awkward. This is often a problem in a book on spirituality and an even greater problem for those translating Scripture and the Church Fathers from the original languages.

Finally, the author is a married lay person who led a "checkered" life for many years following my graced years at the Abbey of Gethsemani. The seeds planted hiddenly at Gethsemani lay dormant and inert, smothered by the allurements of the world. This is of no import except to say that it is expected that books of this kind are written by religious, particularly by religious belonging to one of the contemplative orders (or at least by a Jesuit or Dominican) — those whose "job" is to occasionally undertake a subject as "rarefied and ethereal" as mysticism! Some readers may thereby identify with "one of their own," someone who, perhaps like them, has sometimes "crashed and burned," who has experienced the combat of living a contemplative vocation in a tough and intimidating world, and who, in Merton's words, "has fallen into the same ditch as everyone else."

Anyone who receives My commandments and keeps them will be the one who loves Me. And anyone who loves Me will be loved by My Father, and I shall come and *show myself to them.*

—John 14:21

2

Two Bloodied Words

❦

Any vague sense of spiritual things, any sort of symbolism, any hazily allegorical painting, any poetry which deals with the soul — worse than that, all sorts of superstitions and magical practices — may be and often are described as "mystical."
— *Evelyn Underhill*

"Mysticism," together with its sister word, "contemplation," are the most misunderstood, misapplied, and "bloodied" words in the religious vocabulary. We must then clearly define our terms and retrieve from Christian tradition the true meaning of mysticism and contemplation, as it was experienced and understood by the Church Fathers and those saints who left us writings on the subject.

There are those who think they are mystics because they have read books on different schools of mysticism and are acquainted with their meditation techniques and disciplines — although they practice none of them! Without the praxis, the mystical experience remains but a fancy. Into this same category fall those who have certain psychic abilities (ESP, telepathy, clairvoyance, astral projection, etc.) and are sometimes thought of as mystics. These psychic powers, however, fall not into the realm of spirituality but into that of parapsychology.

Neither should we confuse contemplation and the mystical life with those "exuberant experiences" of saints who were granted visions, locutions, ecstasies, levitations, the power to work miracles — graces that *are* extraordinary (graces *gratis datae*) but are also *inferior* to "ordinary" sanctifying grace and the theological virtues, as St. Thomas and John of the Cross teach.

What, then, is contemplation? St. John of the Cross describes contemplation as "the infused loving knowledge of God." St. Gregory the Great (sixth century) characterizes it as "resting in God... the infused knowledge of God impregnated with love." These two elements, love and knowledge, are always present in the Christian mystical/contemplative experience. To be a mystic is to *experience God in a gifted intuition,* charged with a gentle love and a penetrating, though obscure, knowledge of God.

Although the terms "mysticism" and "contemplation" must often be used when writing on this subject, this experience can also be described as a *gifted Presence* — with a capital "P." This Presence *is passively received* and cannot be induced by any activity or spiritual discipline of our own, *including meditation.* It is therefore called *infused contemplation* and is the only true contemplation, according to ancient Christian tradition.

Although meditation by itself cannot induce contemplation, without a meditation discipline our "inner eye" will never open to the gift. The mystical state, as John of the Cross teaches, is one in which we live in the *habitual loving presence* of God.[1] It is most simply stated by St. Paul: "Before the world was created, he chose us, chose us in Christ... *to live through love in his presence*" (Eph 1:4).

Rodin's statue *The Thinker* is a depiction of the *exact opposite* of contemplation, which has nothing to do with *thinking.* Rather than building on reflective knowledge of revelation, contemplation is a superior knowledge of the heart. This superior knowledge is a *gifted infused Presence* communicated through our intuitive spiritual faculties and cannot be self-induced. To repeat, contemplation is the *normal development of the ordinary Christian life* of sanctifying grace received at baptism, a truth largely ignored by the teaching hierarchy down to the parish level.

Contemplation and the mystical life is not extraordinary except in the sense that relatively few Christians attain to the heights of their faith, attained only, as the Church teaches, in the mystical life. God's seed in us (1 Jn 3:9) is not meant to remain only a seed. God's image, stamped upon our soul, is not intended to remain undeveloped. We are called to "see" that image in "luminous obscurity" and to experience its reality. This "seeing" is called contemplation, a gift that admits of infinite growth, the full flowering of the virtues, accessed only in the mystical life.

> Like Gregory of Nyssa and many other Christian mystics, Rahner holds that progress toward perfection consists in the ever-deepening and more direct awareness of the divine incomprehensibility.
>
> *— Bernard McGinn*[2]

For most Christians the notion of contemplation and the mystical life is far-fetched, ephemeral, misty, airy, fictitious — in a word, unreal. To those who have been gifted with this experience, however, nothing could be more real or more in keeping with their everyday Christian living.

> Contemplation is not only real, but I insist on its simplicity, sobriety, humility, and its integration in normal Christian life. Contemplation should not be exaggerated, distorted or made to seem great. No one can enter into it except by the path of obscurity and self-forgetfulness. He who thinks he knows what it is beforehand prevents himself from finding out the true nature of contemplation. He who thinks that contemplation is lofty and spectacular cannot receive the intuition of a supreme and transcendent Reality which is at the same time immanent in his own ordinary self.
>
> *— Thomas Merton*[3]

Merton reminds us that this gift cannot be satisfactorily explained to anyone who has not some experience of it. "The only way to get rid of misconceptions about contemplation is to experience it."[4]

In the final analysis, after all the metaphors and symbols and analogies have been laid end to end, only the person who has been gifted with this experience can have a true understanding of its reality. However obscure, however delicate, however indefinable, the contemplative nonetheless *knows* with an absolute certitude. "Contemplatives," says George Maloney, "know that they know that they know"! Only the contemplative has a certitude of faith, because this faith is not just the result of a simple intellectual belief but is experientially rooted in the very God who communicates directly to the soul. "Only the contemplative," writes LaGrange, "rises to the heights of faith. This certitude is based on a *secret illumination of the Holy Spirit*" (emphasis added).[5]

Beyond the mediation of ideas, thoughts, words, and concepts, the contemplative "tastes and sees" that the Lord is sweet. This must not be interpreted to suggest that the Christian mystic is "blissed out" all the time! The experience is too deep for that. It is too secret for that. The contemplative still feels pain and anguish and knows sorrow, but with an underlying peace and confidence in Christ. It is the gifted peace of Christ, a peace that the superficial and transient pursuits and pleasures of the world cannot give, no matter how much we immerse ourselves in them.

The great majority of contemplatives live their lives mostly in darkness and aridity, in the darkness of naked faith, knowing God in darkness and therefore, paradoxically, *not* knowing God. The contemplative lives with and within an unspectacular and homely awareness that God simply *is*. Everything that constitutes his or her living is now ordered and joined to this one tremendous reality, this *mysterium tremendum*. Gradually, we become the person for whom Christ once prayed and continues to pray — to be in the world but not of it.

Father, I am not asking you to remove them from the world, but to protect them from the evil one. They do not belong to the world any more than I belong to the world. Consecrate them in truth: your word is truth. . . . I pray not only for these but for those also who through their words will believe in Me.

— John 17:15–20

3

All Who Thirst

❦

Jesus stood there and cried out: "If anyone thirsts, let them come to me! Let them come to me and drink, who believe in me. As scripture says: from their breasts shall flow fountains of living water."

— John 7:37–38

Only those who *thirst* will be given the living waters of contemplation. Only to those who *hunger* will God give himself as food. Desire is the most important ingredient in the quest for the living waters. This desire, however, must be "right" desire, stripped of self-seeking — a desire to love God for God's own sake. Heartfelt desire for God can overarch our weaknesses, our negligences, and even our sins: "Many sins are forgiven her, because she has loved much" (Lk 7:47). Without desire, little progress can be made in the spiritual journey. Without desire, the God of Mercies will remain silent and hidden from our experience. Without desire, the gift of contemplation will never be granted.

Many stifle any possibility of enkindling such desire by constant activity, including, and perhaps most especially, undertaking "works of the Lord." Activity easily can become a form of escapism, causing us to be too outward-minded — a flight from our inner poverty and emptiness, an evasion of coming face to face with our deep selves and our need for healing. We fear silence and solitude because we fear the truth of our inner poverty. Those who attend to their discipline of prayer, however dark and dry, who seek out some silence and solitude in their busy lives, will be gifted with the thirst that will inspire them to long for the living waters of contemplation.

> As the hart pants after the living water, so does my soul long for Thee, O God.
>
> — *Psalm 42:1*

In ancient Palestine, "living water" was understood as running water, water "alive" with freshness and purity. In the Christian and Jewish Scriptures, living water is the symbol for the Holy Spirit, the Spirit that has been "poured forth into our hearts" (Gal 4:6). The Fathers and the saints have always understood "living water" as the gift of contemplation and participation in the mystical life:

> How thirsty one becomes for this thirst! The soul understands the great value of this thirst and, even though the thirst is most painful, it brings with it the very satisfaction by which it is assuaged, in such a way that this is a thirst unquenchable. Indeed, this thirst slakes in such a way that when God satisfies the thirst, the greatest favor He can grant to the soul is to leave it in this same need — and a greater one — to drink the water again.
>
> — *Teresa of Avila*[1]

St. Thomas teaches that God does not bestow the higher gifts of the Holy Spirit because we do not sufficiently desire and ask for them. Merton gives us the reason behind our timidity:

> God seeks Himself in us, and the aridity and sorrow of our heart is the sorrow of God Who is not known to us, Who cannot find Himself in us because we do not dare to believe or trust the incredible truth that He could live in us and live there out of choice, out of preference. We make all this dark

and inglorious because we fail to believe it, we refuse to believe it.

— Thomas Merton[2]

Karl Rahner proposes that over recent centuries our spiritual arteries have become progressively hardened, perhaps even calcified. No longer can we hear the Voice crying out in the desert of our inner wilderness.

Today if you would hear His voice, harden not your heart.

— Psalm 95:8

We harden our hearts not so much by any perversity in our human nature but as a result of being too outwardly focused, oriented to the external world of seemingly endless diversions and ambitions. If our spiritual arteries have become hardened, it is surely because they have been clogged and choked by the stuff of vain and passing pursuits. Meanwhile, "angst" quietly seethes in our bowels, giving rise to various kinds of psychotic behavior and self-destructive actions. The tragedy is we don't realize we are dysfunctional. Since almost everyone else acts the same way, our dysfunction is perceived as "normal"! This inner "angst" also manifests itself in our relentless outward pursuits, in our continual efforts to fill the "metaphysical hole" within us, pursuits that become like dying stars plummeting one after another into a cosmic black hole. We shall find no lasting peace here, no fruitful abiding rest. "The only cure for the angst of modern man," writes Merton, "is mysticism."

In the incessant pursuit of diversion and the consuming drive for money, power, success, and pleasure, modern men and women are hemorrhaging, pouring out their most precious inner vitals upon the unforgiving ground of a false and deceptive quest — a pursuit fueled by society's lie that this is the road to happiness and personal fulfillment. Heedlessly careening along, we do not see the caution signs, especially the one that reads: "Road Ends Ahead!" Blinded by the oncoming twin headlights of ambition and pleasure-seeking, we never see the "Dead End" sign and go merrily skidding off into the ravine.

Many Christians do not feel themselves "worthy" of the higher gifts of the Spirit. This is a false humility and actually reveals a faith that is weak and imperfect. Who is worthy? Worthiness has nothing to do with it. We are loved, not judged. Thousands of "ordinary Christians" — some of whom were once great sinners — are leading the mystical/contemplative life in the world. Christ, who came to heal the ill and the infirm, cured the physically and emotionally diseased while attempting to raise them to higher consciousness. He gave new life to whoever opened themselves to his words; he refused no one. "Whoever comes to me, I will not turn away" (Jn 6:37). We are wont to measure God's generosity by our own rationed-out, stingy kind of benevolence. He has told us otherwise, and with telling force:

> What father among you would hand his son a stone when he asked for bread? Or hand him a snake instead of a fish? Or hand him a scorpion if he asked for an egg? If you then, who are evil know how to give your children what is good, how much more will your heavenly Father give the Holy Spirit to those who ask Him!
>
> — *Luke 11:11–13*

4

The Greatest Sin

Peter, do you love me more than these? ... [then] feed my
sheep ... feed my lambs ... feed my sheep.

—John 21:15

The last words of Our Lord on earth to Peter might well have
been:

Peter, if you love me, lead my sheep to the living water
that I have promised to all who thirst and that I offered the
Samaritan woman at Jacob's Well. Don't get too cerebral,
Peter, for the living water that I will give has little do with the
head but everything to do with the heart. Teach them about
the heart, Peter, that they might worship in spirit and in truth
and become a resurrected people even as they journey on
pilgrimage.

For the first thirteen centuries or so of Christianity, contemplation was considered the normal goal and development
of the Christian life, for both religious and laity. Following
the Reformation, into the eighteenth-century Age of Reason
and the nineteenth-century Age of Enlightenment, the contemplative heritage of the Church was displaced by excessive
rational thinking and an overworked speculative theology
that became "the faith." It is a disease with us still:

Today we see in every religion an inherent danger whereby
the faithful are allowed to settle for the trappings ... instead

of continuing to grow through an intensive searching in one's
heart for the wild God of the desert who cannot be put
into convenient boxes of concepts and doctrines. Western
theology by and large has become reduced to a static form of
objectifying God's transcendence.

— George A. Maloney[1]

With the exception of scattered monasteries and a hand-
ful of mystic writers, the Christian contemplative heritage
was all but lost and consigned to dusty remote archives.
(Grounded in the Greek and Oriental Church Fathers
and untouched by the Protestant Reformation,[2] the Eastern Church never lost its contemplative orientation and
vision.)

"Now with the advent of cross-cultural dialogue and historical research" writes Thomas Keating, "the Christian contemplative tradition has begun anew." This is evidenced
by the growing number of spiritual writers espousing the
contemplative/mystical life for all who would desire and seek
it, some of whom are quoted or referred to in this book. It
is evidenced also by the growing number of people and small
communities who are faithful practitioners of different ways
of contemplative prayer and who have come to know the
Lord by *an experience of his presence.*

Since the Middle Ages the Western Church has often prof-
fered a stale and nutritionless substitute for the living waters
of contemplation. It has come to us prepackaged and carefully filtered — a diet of dry declarations and statements that
we are asked (sometimes told) to chew upon until spiritual
sclerosis clogs the arteries to our hearts. Many are the sins of
the Church over the centuries, up to the present day. None
compares, however, to that of restricting her children to a
diet of tasteless spiritual morsels cooked up in the ovens of
left-brain theology.

Our obligation as His ministers is not only to invite and
encourage souls, but to oblige them to enter into the great

banquet of the nuptials of the Lamb. If we act otherwise, we
are traitors or at least disloyal servants, depriving Him of the
delights He finds in dwelling with the sons of men.
                                    — *Juan Gonzales Arintero, O.P.*[3]

When we inquire why those appointed to be the shepherds
of our souls do not gather us together and instruct us in the
school of the Spirit, it must be regrettably concluded that
few have knowledge and experience in the contemplative/
mystical life. Why is it that we are not instructed in the ways
of meditation *as central to personal and parish life*, without which a profound, contemplative spirituality cannot be
accessed?

Our parishes, especially larger ones, have programs and
committees for everything under the sun, except ongoing
training in the art of meditation, without which the "inner
eye" of the soul cannot open to the Reality within it. Centuries before Christ, the sages of the East intuited this
transforming truth and so taught their disciples. The Desert
and early Church Fathers also understood that without a
discipline of imageless, wordless prayer the spiritual life
would remain purely on intellectual and psychological levels and never radically convert our hearts, never transform
and awaken our true inner being.

Programs, including Bible study programs (which are pri-
marily exegetical), however useful and valuable, are nonetheless secondary to the spiritual life and peripheral to one's
inner growth and development. We might ask: "Have our
parishes become one big program?" Until our appointed
shepherds lead their flocks into the art of "prayer of the
heart" everything will remain pretty much the way it has
been over recent centuries — parishes incapable of leading
people to deep personal inner transformation, the source of
authentic Church renewal.

Where are there still the "spiritual fathers," the Christian
gurus, who possess the charisma of initiating into meditation

and even into mysticism in which man's ultimate reality —
union with God — is accepted as a holy courage? Where
are the people who have the courage to be disciples of such
spiritual fathers?

— *Karl Rahner*[4]

Rahner's vision of the future Church (shared by Merton) is
a "Church of the little flock," a Church that will witness the
defection of large numbers of perfunctory Catholics. What
will remain are remnants or "little flocks" of true Christians
of deep faith and prayer who will, over time, rekindle and
renew the Church — a Church, in Rahner's words, "of real
spirituality."

As has been often said, religion has to do with doing, with
the externals. Spirituality has to do with being, with the mysterious inner self. Religion often divides humankind, even
to the extent of fomenting hatred, wars, and incalculable
human suffering. Spirituality, on the other hand — of whatever deep and sincere kind — heals and unites and makes
us all brothers and sisters, since true spirituality intuits and
honors the common ground of all being.

The teaching Church, from top to bottom, appears gen-
erally willing to accept a status quo that blesses simple
intellectual faith and the following of external forms but does
not, in practice, truly believe each of us is called to experiential union with God in this life. We chew on the rind and
never taste the savory, transforming fruit it hides. We never
evolve into people of fire (which has little to do with emotions). This fire, which Christ came to cast upon the earth, is
lit in each person one by one. It is like that witnessed by a little boy I once knew. Enchanted by fire, he struck a match to
a single blade of dry grass in a field. To his great surprise and
astonishment, he watched blade after blade become a field of
fire altering the face of the earth.

Attending liturgies and receiving the sacraments is not
a substitute for taking serious personal responsibility for
our spiritual life, signified by our commitment to a disci-

pline of prayer and meditation. They are complementary and should work together, as a unity, in building up the body of Christ who we are, individually and as a people. Each of us must climb the mountain before us essentially alone, albeit helped and supported by our Church, our spiritual soul-mates, brothers and sisters who together are plodding pilgrims on the spiritual journey.

If we reflect back over the sermons and homilies we have heard over the years, we will realize that, almost without exception, they have dealt with how we are to conduct ourselves (the moral virtues). Yet it is contemplation that radically strengthens the moral virtues, which inspires us to practice them, and that vivifies and perfects them.

The contemplative needs no sermon or catechism to instruct him or her on how to respond to God's will, which is concretely imbedded in the daily events of life itself. The gift of contemplation anoints us with the unction of the Holy Spirit — God made real and vital to our experience. To the recollected and receptive contemplative, the Spirit manifests herself[5] instantly with each of life's encounters, gently prompting and prodding us at each moment, our constant Teacher. This anointing remains always with us, ever deepening, ever divinizing us.

> You have not lost the anointing He gave you, and you do not need anyone to teach you. The anointing He gave teaches you everything. (1 Jn 2:27).

It is the mystical life that fires and animates the Body of Christ. Without this fire burning in its members, this Body will never "become the perfect Man, fully mature with the fullness of Christ himself" (Eph 4:13). This fire can be lit only from deep within, at our "core center" where the "Divine Spark" (Eckhart) awaits our disinfection from worldly attachments and pursuits and the turning upside down of our value systems.

The words of Thomas Keating may come as a disturbing revelation to Christians, particularly those diligently working in the service of the Lord:

> Without the experience of "resting in God" [contemplation], all the capital sins are flourishing without one actually being aware of the fact. One may think one is doing great things for God if one gets into parochial work or teaching, but the seven capital sins — the results of the emotional programs for happiness — are there in concrete form.[6]

Thomas Keating reminds us that our emotional programs for happiness, first developed in early childhood, cannot possibly succeed. Our need for a sense of achievement, of "doing good," our secret desire for recognition and approval are all rooted in the false ego-self, the "home" of the seven capital sins. Despite our good intentions, our work is polluted with the residual fallout of the capital sins, a dysfunction requiring the profound purifying action of God. If we are to become contemplatives, God alone must prepare our hearts for this new in-pouring of the Holy Spirit and create a fitting abode for the coming of the Bridegroom. God, and only God, must prune the tree.

However, we must not interpret Keating to mean that our deeds and actions have no value or worth in the eyes of God, only that they are infected by self. It is according to the depth of our sincerity and pure motivation — or what a Buddhist might describe as emanating from "pure heart" — that the coin of our actions is stamped with a Christ-likeness:

> Insofar as our spiritual life consists of thoughts, desires, actions, devotions and projects of our exterior self, it participates in the non-being and falsity of that exterior self. No matter how external our spiritual life may be, if it has a root of sincerity, it is based in the interior person and therefore has value and reality in the sight of God. But the purpose of our life is to bring all our strivings and desires into the

sanctuary of the true inner self and place them all under the
command of an inner and God-inspired consciousness. This
is the work of grace.

— *Thomas Merton*[7]

There is no other way for us to be radically cleansed, John
of the Cross reminds us, except by walking the *Via Dolorosa*
that leads through the passive, purifying dark nights. *"They
must pass this way,"* asserts John of the Cross, referring to
the night of sense, *"to be perfect, that is, to attain the divine union of the soul with God."*[8] All our ascetic efforts
will otherwise fall far short of effecting that radical cleansing that the Desert fathers called "purity of heart," allowing
our "inner eye" to see God. "Happy the pure of heart, for
they shall see God." Without the "divine therapy" our faith
will remain weak and our pursuit of virtue will be frustrated
and short-circuited.

Without contemplation we shall never make much progress
in virtue, and shall never be fitted to make others advance
therein. We shall never entirely rid ourselves of our weaknesses and imperfections. We shall remain always bound to
earth and shall never rise much above mere natural feelings.
We shall never be able to render to God perfect service. But
with contemplation, we shall effect more both for ourselves
and for others in a month than we should accomplish in ten
years without it.

— *Louis Lallemant*[9]

5

The Testimony of Jung

❧

I find that all my thoughts circle round God, like the planets around the sun, and are as irresistibly attracted by Him. I would feel it to be the grossest sin if I were to oppose any resistance . . . this force.

— Carl Jung

At what stage of his life Jung "became a mystic" is obscure. That he became a mystic is verified by his later writings. Toward the end of his rich and productive life, Jung was interviewed by the BBC. The interviewer asked: "Dr. Jung, you are the son of a Protestant minister. Do you still believe in God?" Jung calmly took a long puff from his curled pipe and replied: "No." One could almost hear a collective gasp among the TV viewing audience. Jung paused again, taking a long draught from his pipe. Quite matter of factly he added: "I know."

Jung's minister father had never known a religious experience that would verify his Christian faith. Jung wrote of his father's doubts, which gnawed away at him and undermined his faith. Possessed only of an intellectual faith, his father would often dismiss his young son's probing queries with "You must have faith" — a response hardly sufficient for this keen, inquisitive mind. Once, when they came to the section on the Trinity in the syllabus his father was using for instruction, his father said: "We will pass over this sec-

41

tion — it is not important"! The young boy subsequently lost all interest in pursuing further instruction.

At the age of seventy, Jung would write in a letter:

> It is of the highest importance that the educated and enlightened should know religious truth as something living in the soul, and not as an obtuse and unreasonable relic of the past.[1]

"It is high time," Jung wrote, "that we realize *it is pointless to praise the light if nobody can see it!*" (emphasis added).[2]

(The Eastern Church has always insisted on the importance of *personal experience,* not simply the intellectual acceptance of doctrine, dogma, rules, and externals. Accordingly, Orthodoxy regards persons without experiential knowledge as "second-hand Christians." Orthodoxy teaches that all authentic Christian life must be rooted in the mystical).

A well-known excerpt from Dr. Jung's voluminous writings is worth repeating here:

> During the past thirty-five years people from all the civilized countries of the earth have consulted me. I have treated many hundreds of patients, the larger number being Protestants, a smaller number of Jews and not more than five or six believing Catholics. Among all my patients that were in the second half of life — that is, over thirty-five — there has not been one whose problem in the last resort was not that of finding a religious outlook on life. It is safe to say that every one of them fell ill because they had lost what the living religions of every age give to their followers — and none of them has been really healed who did not regain their religious outlook.[3]

George Maloney states that, given exceptions, a person should not begin to think about contemplation until around middle age. In other words, we need to digest a thick slice of life, its ups and downs, its trials and disappointments,

its realities and falsities so as to have accumulated sufficient maturity and life experience to competently integrate
the realities of the contemplative journey.

Central to Jungian thought is his concept of self, which
Jung understood to be our total personality and "core center." As Christopher Bryan points out, "Jung's concept of the
self, as he was well aware, accords closely with the Christian
mystical tradition:

> The spiritual guides who stand in this tradition teach that
> God who is present everywhere is most surely to be found
> [experienced] within the individual's own soul; and it is here
> that he is most accessible.[4]

Jung states that without the personal discovery of the
immanent God, we are subject to the loss of our person:

> The individual who is not anchored in God can offer no
> resistance on his own resources to the physical and moral
> blandishments of the world. For this we need the evidence of
> *inner transcendent experience* which alone can protect us
> from the otherwise inevitable submersion in the mass. Merely
> intellectual or even moral insight into the stultification and
> moral irresponsibility of the mass is a *negative recognition*
> and amounts to not much more than a wavering on the road
> to the atomization of the individual. It lacks the driving force
> of religious conviction, *since it is merely rational* [emphasis
> added].[5]

Jung poses the consideration: "Christ is in us and we in
Him. Why should the activity and the presence of the Son of
Man within us not be *real and knowable?*"

The writings of the great Swiss psychologist offer weighty
empirical evidence that our peace, our happiness, our wholeness, *our individuation,* depend upon the discovery of the
Divine indwelling — "in whom we live and breathe and have

our being" (Acts 17:28). For Jung, this is not only a matter of supreme importance but also an occasion of thanksgiving:

> Every day I am thankful to God that I have been given to experience the reality of the Divine image within me. Had this not been granted to me I should have indeed been a bitter enemy of Christianity and especially of the Church. But thanks to this act of grace my life has meaning and my inward eye has been opened to the beauty and greatness of dogma.[6]

6

Many Are Called

❦

There was a man who gave a great banquet and invited a large
number of people. When the time for the banquet came, he
sent his servant to say to those who had been invited: "Come
along, everything is ready now." But all alike started to make
excuses.

— Luke 14:16–18

The Church Fathers and the saints often commented on the
words of Christ "Many are called, but few are chosen," ap-
plying them to the mystical life. To be *called* and to be *chosen*
are not the same. One who is called has been extended the invitation and is free to accept or "make excuses." One chosen
has *responded* to the invitation, "returning the RSVP" with
gratitude along with a commitment to generously undertake
whatever is required to be admitted to the banquet.

Implied in the word "many" is the implication that *all*
Christians are called to a contemplative spirituality. Teresa
of Avila reminds us that Christ invited *all* who thirst to come
to him to drink of the living waters, and did so loudly (Jn
7:38). The invitation, however, is extended only to those who
thirst for the living waters and who generously take upon
themselves the *praxis* (asceticism) that will prepare them for
the gift.

Though few perhaps may bring to full maturity the seeds of
contemplation implanted in their hearts by Christian faith, it

45

still remains possible for them to do so with the help of the Holy Spirit even in the midst of the world.

— Thomas Merton[1]

We are nonetheless mindful of those whose life situations may make it impossible, or at least extraordinarily difficult, first to hear and then to answer the call. Some live in inhuman, even agonizing conditions and surroundings; some are mentally or psychologically maimed. There are others who hear the call but faintly only to have it drowned out by the constant static and din of worldly cares and concerns. There is also mystery here, reasons that cannot be easily explained why some hear and answer the call and others do not. It is not for us here to probe the reasons *why not* but to look at some of the reasons why many *are* called although few are chosen.

A question often posed is this: "Are not special and extraordinary graces required for the mystical life?" Following the Church Fathers, St. Thomas and St. John of the Cross (Doctors of the Church) say *no* and say so emphatically. Quite the contrary since, as they teach, the mystical/contemplative life is in the *normal development of ordinary Christian life.*

> The grace of the virtues and of the gifts suffices in itself by its normal development to dispose us to the mystical life. Mystical contemplation is necessary for the full perfection of the Christian life.
>
> *— Reginald Garrigou-LaGrange*[2]

In other words, *experience* is the important thing, an experience built upon and dependent upon faith.

If you and I were one of a countless variety of flowers in a field, each with its own unique fragrance and beauty, and if, as flowers, we were possessed of a reflective consciousness, no one would have to tell us that our uniqueness, our fragrance, our special beauty — indeed our very existence —

was the mineral-rich ground in which we were rooted, freely watered from on high. No one would have to tell us that we came forth from a tiny seed, awaiting the life-giving rains to blossom into glorious fullness.

So, too, contemplatives need no one to tell them that God is their loving Mother-Father, that we are grounded and sourced in God and nourished by God and given our beauty by God. For the contemplative experiences all this and is filled with awe and gratitude. The contemplative knows *experientially* that he or she is the unique offspring, the special *love-child* of God. This certitude is established in the contemplative by the direct infused communication and illumination of the Holy Spirit in our hearts:

> The Spirit and our spirit give united witness that we are children of God.
>
> — *Romans 8:16*

7

Few Are Chosen

ᏧᏍᎳᎧ

> Some persons talk about mysticism but misunderstand it and
> abuse it. Others, far greater in number, are altogether ignorant
> of mysticism and apparently wish to remain so. They aim only
> at the common virtues and do not tend to perfection, which
> they consider too lofty.
>
> — *Reginald Garrigou-LaGrange*

If there are few contemplatives in our parishes it is because
most are content to remain "conventional Christians." Conventional Christians secretly assure themselves that if they
attend to the prescribed externals, go regularly to church,
and don't go off the deep end, they are pleasing to God
(although in fact they are pleasing mostly to themselves).
Nonetheless, we *are* called to "go off the deep end" by aban-
doning ourselves to the Lord's care and to risk everything
by letting go of everything. We are invited (though never de-
manded) to hang over an *interior abyss* in dark trusting faith
where our security blanket of control is stripped away and
we stand naked and defenseless before our Creator. Such is
the essential nature of the contemplative/mystical experience.

Theologians speak of the "general or remote" call to the
mystical life, the call implanted at baptism by sanctifying
grace, and the "proximate or individual" call, which we
later "hear" if we are faithful to God's word and his grace.
Our response is inexorably tied to our freedom to accept or
refuse the call. The invitation is tendered many times in our

lives until, after an indeterminate number of refusals, God may withdraw the invitation, seeing we are not interested. St. Francis de Sales tells us that "this benevolence is offered by means of invitations, urgings and pleadings, but without any force or violence."[1] So also St. Teresa:

> His Mercy is so great that he hinders no one from drinking from the fountain of life. Indeed, He calls us loudly to do so (Jn 7:37). But He is so good that He will not force us to drink of it.
>
> — *Teresa of Avila*[2]

The gift of contemplation is denied those whose lives are largely outward and external, lives eaten up with endless activity (religious as well as secular), curiosity, pleasure, and ambition. Without extended moments of quiet reflection and silence, we will never hear the Voice calling us from deep within. For this Voice to be heard we must have "ears to hear" that are lodged in the heart. Our hearts cannot "hear" through the din and turmoil of a constantly busy exterior life. The sweet strains of a violin cannot be heard amid the blaring of trumpets. But once the call is heard (it may take many "intonations"!) it must be answered with seriousness and generosity. It must be received with the certain knowledge that grace accompanies it, that grace will smooth the way, that God's grace will never fail us. We must rely on this truth much more than upon our own poor efforts, which we are very much tempted to do at first:

> If we demand too little of ourselves, this is because we do not count sufficiently on grace, because we do not sufficiently ask for it. If our spiritual life declines to a lower level and if we are satisfied with an entirely natural life, this is a consequence of our believing we are alone in acting, forgetting that God is in us and with us.
>
> — *Reginald Garrigou-LaGrange*[3]

The "divine spark" within us remains only a spark for as long as we are content to let it simply flicker in unattended isolation. God profoundly desires this spark be ignited in us and brightly burn, awaiting the conversion of our hearts to enkindle it. We must know that God seeks us with a mighty stirring. "For God patiently puts up with the people who make him angry...for the sake of those other people...to whom he wants to reveal the richness of His glory. *We are those people!*" (Rom 9:23). Paul reminds us we are not alone in our quest: "It is God for his own loving purpose who puts both the will and the action into you" (Phil 2:13).

The invitation to the mystical life is never extended to those who do not desire it or who do not dispose their lives to receive the gift. "Few of us," Teresa of Avila reminds us, "dispose ourselves that God may communicate it [contemplation] to us."[4] This is a dark tragedy, for in failing to dispose ourselves for the gift, we reject the enormous possibilities for our own joy and happiness. The grandeur of the Christian calling is thereby marginalized to living the ordinary common life.

> Many will not develop enough spirituality to be suitably prepared for the mystical life. This is due primarily to a lack of humility, purity of heart, simplicity of inward gaze, recollection and generosity — or because they are too naturally inclined to be outward minded. *They do not love the silent and profound prayer which leads to union* [emphasis added].
>
> — *Reginald Garrigou-LaGrange*[5]

Having received the invitation, many flee from what is required for the invitation to take root:

> Others who as a rule are more advanced will be called to the mystical life in a proximate manner but will not respond to this call. Many will become discouraged after their first steps in the Dark Night. This last group is numerous and, according

to John of the Cross, in this difficult passage they are also
badly directed.

— Reginald Garrigou-LaGrange[6]

If "few are chosen" it is not because God chooses to deny
the gift. Rather, we choose to decline the invitation, finding
countless excuses and rationalizations why we cannot attend
the banquet, foremost of which is needless activity and excessive diversion. It will be attended by others more generous,
more desirous of union with God. Let us not be among those
who, through laziness and lukewarmness, refuse to make the
effort that will dispose us for the gift, nor among those who,
having received the invitation, find every excuse not to attend
the banquet. We can know with certainty that our small efforts will find grace supporting and strengthening us on all
sides, providing both "the will and the action." For every
ounce of effort we extend as our cooperative part, Bounti-
ful Mercy will pour out grace a hundredfold. "Glory be to
him whose power working in us can do infinitely more than
we can ask or imagine" (Eph 3:20).

The gift awaits us, *held in our name,* a divine "layaway
plan" awaiting presentation of our "claim check," our decision to seek it. We must knock persistently, as did the
importunate friend of the Gospel (Lk 11:5–8). Unless we "cut
and run," the gift is already ours! But we must begin, we
must take that first important grace-charged step:

The beginning is the more important part... and if that
person should do no more than take one step, the step will
itself contain so much power that we will not have to fear
losing it, nor will we fail to be very well paid.

— Teresa of Avila[7]

8

Beyond Church

❧

The Church is not about laws, doctrines, morals or politics. These are secondary, as are rubrics, popes, priests. The Church is about life: ours and God's, as focused in Jesus. Ah, God, if You are boring, we have missed You. Nothing is so real as You, nothing so living. The fault is not with God. Jesus could not be better.

— *John Carmody*

The birthing of the Son in us, remarks Meister Eckhart, is the greatest joy of the Father. This "birthing" is a dynamic process from infancy to maturity, from the postwomb state of "sucklings" nurtured by the milk of discursive prayer and consolations, to spiritual adulthood nourished by the strong meat of mysticism.

Thomas Keating reminds us that the "three presences" in the liturgy are meant to lead us to a living awareness of the indwelling Trinity. Christ is present in the congregation (wherever two or three are gathered), in the proclamation of "the Word," and in the Real Presence of the Eucharist — or as Orthodoxy expresses it, in the "Mysteries." These three manifestations of Emmanuel, God with us, are meant to awaken us to the Divine Presence within.

Bede Griffiths, one of the great Christian mystics of our century, tells the story of a school in India with Hindu and Catholic children. One day the children were asked: "Where is God?" All the Catholic children pointed to the sky. All the Hindu youngsters pointed to their hearts.

A remarkable ancient manuscript by an anonymous Syrian has been recently discovered. Entitled "The Book of Degrees," it was written not for monks but for lay people. On the basis of internal evidence, it seems that the author was an ascetic of the early fourth century. Apparently, he was the contemporary of the great St. Antony of the Desert and the beginnings of early organized monasticism.[1]

This Syrian writer stresses the importance for Christians to "pass beyond" the Visible Church and enter the Church of the Heart and then the Church on High. He sketches out a three-tiered edifice; at the lower level is the Visible Church of externals. He observed that, even in his day, most Christians are "stuck" in this lower Church and never progress beyond its structures and externals.

The author writes of two higher Churches to which the Christian should aspire, the Church of the Heart, which only some enter, and, finally, the Church on High, entered by the few. This ancient scribe insists, however, that we must not sever our ties with the Visible Church and go off on our own, "up into the mountains" as he puts it. It is the Visible Church that makes it possible for us to climb to the upper stories of this three-tiered edifice.

> Without this Visible Church no one will enter the Church of the Heart or the Church on High. If anyone cuts himself off from the Visible Church and goes into the mountains to pray (as a permanent state), he is guilty and in error.

The Visible Church, he writes, "brings forth her children like infants which suck milk until they are weaned," a nurturing "staging area" for passage to the higher Churches. Our writer also refers to the three "Churches" as three "liturgies," which interpenetrate and "respond unceasingly to each other within the life of the Church."

> Let us not scorn, then, the Visible Church, for she makes her
> children grow. Neither let us scorn the Church of the Heart
> for she strengthens the weak. But let us have an earnest
> desire for the Church on High, which perfects all the saints.

(It is interesting that St. John of the Cross, twelve centuries later, also refers to beginners as "sucklings" still at the breast on the mother's milk of discursive prayer and meditation.)

The author alludes to "a hidden prayer of the heart which clings to the Lord and meditates unceasingly upon Him [contemplation]...the heart becoming the altar of a spiritual and interior sacrifice and liturgy." Having once gained entrance to the Church of the Heart, we are urged to ascend to the Church on High — where one "hears the harmonies of heaven, an ineffable liturgy which transcends all that human speech may utter." Few enter here, for this presupposes a radical kenosis, or self-emptying, and a total purification of the heart.

One cannot escape the analogy between the "three Churches" and the classic three stages of the spiritual life (first enumerated by Origen in the second century): the purgative way of beginners, the way of proficients or the way of contemplatives, and the unitive way, the way of the perfect. This ascent is proportionate to growth in prayer that becomes ever more simple, evolving into a profound interiorization and simplicity of inward gaze and having an energizing life-rhythm of its own.

Sometimes the three stages of the spiritual life are misinterpreted as distinct, hermetically sealed-off compartments of the spiritual life. To employ an analogy, they are sometimes viewed as clearly defined "states" such as one might encounter traveling through New Mexico, then across the border into Arizona, then into the paradisiacal state of California! Like the three "Churches" of our Syrian author, the three stages of the spiritual journey interpenetrate, just as the leaf is always part of the branch and the branch always part of the trunk. These designations are intended to indicate that one of these states predominates, but is not mutually exclusive of the others. (We need always remember that progress in Christian perfection consists not in contemplation but in charity, which contemplation profoundly vivifies and perfects).

Whoever our anonymous Syrian writer was, he evidences the ancient and consistent teaching tradition of the Fathers and the saints — that *all are called* to an experiential penetration of our faith, to experience our faith in "luminous obscurity." If, year after year after year, we have been faithful children of the Visible Church, should we not at some time, in some quiet reflective moment, have ever asked ourselves: "Is that all there is?"

> If God's essence is love, He seeks by His nature to share His being by communicating His presence. God becomes a God-toward-others by communicating Himself through His Word and His Spirit of love. God creates the whole world as good, as a sign of His burning desire to *give Himself in faithful communication through His Word* [emphasis added].
>
> — *George A. Maloney*[2]

9

Called into God's Own Life

❦

> One who diligently studies the depths of the mystery of the
> Trinity receives secretly in his spirit a moderate amount of
> understanding of God's nature, yet he is unable to clearly
> explain in words the ineffable depth of this mystery. As, for in-
> stance, how the same thing is capable of being numbered and
> yet rejects numeration, how it is observed with distinctions yet
> is understood as one, how it is separate as to personality yet
> is not divided as to subject matter.
>
> — *Gregory of Nyssa*

As the mystical life deepens, the contemplative is gifted with
a subtle, gentle, obscure yet nonetheless most real infused
loving knowledge of the Holy Trinity. The Three Divine Persons manifest themselves intuitively present in their uniqueness as Persons yet always undivided, distinct yet never
separated, individual in their self-revelation yet always one.
Living experientially in the mystery of the Trinity is the
summit of the Christian faith, to which all are called.

> How absolutely sad that Jesus Christ wishes to lead us into
> the presence of the Holy Trinity as the source and ultimate
> center of all reality and, yet, we Christians, in general, remain
> ignorant of this truth.
>
> — *George Maloney*[1]

As many in actual practice appear to believe, Jesus Christ
is not the culmination of the Christian faith, but is, as he de-

scribed himself, "the way" to the Father, in the love-bond of
the Holy Spirit. Because the eternal Word became flesh and
"pitched his tent among us," Jesus Christ became the *Pontifex Maximus,* the great bridge between heaven and earth,
God and humankind. Only Jesus Christ, through the Spirit,
can lead us into the divine community of triune love. "No
one comes to the Father *unless I draw him*" (Jn 14:6). "No
one has ever seen God; it is the only Son who is in the bosom
of the Father *who has made him known*" (Jn 1:18). "No one
knows the Father except the Son and those to whom the Son
chooses to reveal him" (Mt 11:17).

> Although, like all other mysteries, the Incarnation flows from
> the highest of all, the mystery of the Trinity, yet with regard
> to us, the Incarnation is the most important of all because it
> is through Christ that we are incorporated in the life of the
> three Divine Persons and receive into our hearts the Holy
> Spirit, the bond of perfection, Who unites us to God with the
> same Love which unites the Father and the Son.
>
> — *Thomas Merton*[2]

Christianity honors and exalts the person, our true self.
Jesus came that our deepest true inner self might be awakened to new life and have life more abundantly (Jn 10:10),
partaking of God's very own life (2 Pet 1:4). The Divine
Personhoods are the source and ground of our own creaturely personhoods, having been created in God's image by
an act of pure self-giving love. As Christians, we are called to
an ever-deepening realization and ongoing consciousness of
this truth:

> Life is meant to be an ongoing process of knowing and
> loving, of experiencing profoundly the Father and the Son in
> the Spirit. We cannot know the inner nature of God unless it
> be revealed through God communicating this truth through
> the Word, Jesus Christ, and his Spirit.
>
> — *George A. Maloney*[3]

Karl Rahner has written that if the doctrine of the Trinity were to be removed from Catholic Church dogma and teaching, few would miss it. Rahner states that most Catholics, in practice, really believe in tri-theism, three Gods, and not in the Trinity of three persons in one nature.[4] Eastern Orthodoxy, rooted in the theology of the Eastern and Oriental Fathers, has always been profoundly Trinitarian. The Orthodox Divine Liturgy is resplendent with continuous prayers, hymns, and acclamations to the Holy Trinity, so much so that the worshiper is inescapably imbued with the reality of the living Father, Son, and Spirit.

A life consciously lived in Christ, in the three Persons of the one God, is the decisive mark that distinguishes (but does not separate!) the Christian from the non-Christian mystic. Here, divergence and convergence co-exist. Religion has largely to do with "doing"; spirituality has to do with "being." This is why the religionist can be destitute of a substantive spirituality. It is also why men and women of deep spirituality, without surrendering or forfeiting their foundational teachings and precepts, are able to transcend them and profoundly communicate with others of different spiritual paths.

At the deepest core-center of all humankind there is an ineffable, inviolable truth, called by different names, that attracts, heals, inspires, and unites — a truth beyond our ability to dissect and clearly articulate. It is a communion of spirit:

> The deepest level of communication is not communication, but communion. It is wordless. It is beyond words and it is beyond speech and beyond concepts. Not that we discover a new unity. We discover an older unity. My dear brothers and sisters, we are already one, but we imagine that we are not. What we have to recover is our original unity. What we have to be — is what we are.
>
> — *Thomas Merton*[5]

As someone has correctly observed, those on different spiritual paths are not climbing different sides of the same mountain, but are scaling *different mountains*. We nonetheless suggest that these different mountains are part of the *same mountain range,* whose skyward peaks aspire to ultimate truth, experienced subjectively — mountains stretching upward out of diverse theological, historical, and cultural ground. Consequently, as the ascent progresses, the "interior view" of each is not experienced in the same way, though each is ineffable and ultimately incommunicable. It is precisely this "ineffable ground" that binds together all people of genuine spirituality, regardless of the diversity of their spiritual paths. The one "divine spark" burns within every human being, recognized as such or not.

Thomas Merton found more in common with many mystics he met in Asia than with most of his Christian contemporaries back home, encountering them on the ground of deep personal experience. Merton writes that if Christianity is to pursue fruitful dialogue with other great spiritual paths, it must be the mystic who speaks for Christianity rather than the dogmatist who is "walled in" by the boundaries of doctrine, walls that tend to cleave and separate rather than unite and heal. The experiential life of the Christian mystic makes it possible to share common touchstones of truth with his or her non-Christian counterpart — however impossible these touchstones may be to articulate precisely.

Just as there are "many [different] rooms in my Father's house" (Jn 14:2), so too are there different "mountains" we must scale according to our chosen committed paths. For the Christian, the summit of the journey is experiential life in the mystery of Father, Son, and Spirit, one God.

> If anyone loves me they will keep my word, and my Father will love them, and we shall come to them and make our home with them. The Advocate, the Holy Spirit, whom the Father will send in my name, will teach you everything.
> — *John 14:23, 26*

We do not possess, as we often believe, our own private "reservoir" of love. It is because God is Love and has planted his seed in us (1 Jn 3:9) that we "genetically inherit," so to speak, a capacity for love by which we are able to love others. Our capacity for love, therefore, admits of no bounds, what Karl Rahner calls "the inexhaustible transcendence of man." In contrast to Aquinas's static definition of the human being as a "rational animal," the early Eastern Church Father St. Irenaeus describes humankind as a "possibility for growth." Rooted in God, we have the potential to continually grow and become totally selfless love, that is, to become "perfect as our heavenly Father is perfect" (Mt 5:48). In the idiom of the Eastern Fathers, this process is called "divinization."

Not to be open to God's love and thereby to refuse it is to commit the ultimate sin against ourselves. In so doing, we condemn ourselves to a shrivelled-up life of consuming self-serving interests and motives, a life cramped in upon itself while we attempt to squeeze out whatever pleasures and gratifications we can "to make ourselves happy."

> Sin is the refusal of the spiritual life. In a word, sin is the
> refusal of God's will and of his love. It is more radically
> a refusal to be what we are, a rejection of our mysterious,
> contingent, spiritual reality hidden in the very mystery of God.
> — *Thomas Merton*[6]

By distancing ourselves from God — and thereby from our own true inner self — we deny our own deepest potentialities and fulfillment, the true happiness we desperately seek, but seek wrongly.

As we faithfully tread the spiritual journey, God is re-creating and renewing us at every instant, though we never "see" it (Mk 4:26–28). If we continue faithful to the journey, we will come to "know the love of Christ which is beyond all [intellectual] knowledge until we are filled with the utter fullness of God (Eph 3:19). We can have faith that God will bring us to full being, to full personhood, because of him who sacrificed himself for us: "Since God did not spare his own Son but gave him up for the benefit of all, we may be certain that after such a gift that he will not refuse us anything he can give" (Rom 8:32).

> Batter my heart, three-personed God, for you
> as yet but knock, breathe, shine and seek to mend;
> That I may rise, and stand, o'erthrow me. and bend
> your force, to break, blow, burn and make me new.
> Take us to you, imprison me, for I, except you
> enthrall me, shall never be free; nor even chaste,
> except you ravish me.
>
> *— John Donne*

Part Two

Contemplative Prayer: Beyond Words and Images

10

The Primacy of Prayer

❦

Many have entered the Kingdom without the sacraments.
None has entered without prayer.
> — *Karl Rahner*

Without a discipline of prayer, without extended intervals of
silence and solitude in our busy lives, contemplation will remain an unrealized sentiment. The living waters come to us
over the aqueduct of prayer. As soon as we make the commitment to a prayer discipline, our lives begin to change almost
immediately, for the waters of grace come quickly trickling
down.

The goal and objective of prayer is to bring us into an ever-
deepening experiential awareness that Christ is the "Soul
of our soul," to awaken us to this reality and to effect an
ongoing transformation of consciousness that God is the
ground and source of our being.

Prayer has but one function: to bring us to a personal
experiential awareness of our union with God in Christ,
a transformation of consciousness... an awakening of the
presence of God within us.

Our life is a continuous seeking of God and finding Him by
love, and sharing that love with other people. In prayer, we
become aware of our inner true self.
> — *Thomas Merton*[1]

It is only in deep, silent "prayer of the heart" that we are gifted with an awareness of our true inner being. At some depth point our self ceases to experience itself as its own center, for it has become God-centered; God is now experienced as its inmost living core, the still point of the turning world, both ours within and that without. This gift brings with it an absolute certitude that God *is* and that our own self is immersed in a Self that is transcendent and, paradoxically, at the same time closer to us than we are to ourselves.

Gradually, day by day, we put on the "mind of Christ" (1 Cor 2:16), whose will, more and more, becomes our will and whose love, more and more, becomes our love by which we are able to love ourselves and love others.

> By God's doing Christ has become our wisdom, and our
> virtue, and our holiness, and our freedom.
> — *1 Corinthians 1:30*

Habitual aliveness to the reality of this deepest Christ-I is what is called the gift of contemplation. It is expressed most simply and profoundly by St. Paul: "I live, now no longer I, but Christ lives in me" (Gal 2:27).

When starting out, some may need to pray the written prayers of others and employ their meditations. As soon as we are able, our prayer should become our own — simple, personal, humble, and heartfelt, bereft of fanciful, artfully constructed language and lofty ideas.

> Pray in all simplicity. . . . The publican and the thief were
> reconciled by a single utterance. In your prayers there is no
> need for high-flown words, for it is the simple babblings of
> children that have more often won the heart of the Father of
> Heaven.
> — *St. John Climacus*[2]

There are too many books and methods on prayer that tend to make prayer difficult and complicated. In recent times prayer has often been made into a science of formulas and methods with detailed prescriptions and laborious techniques. It was not always so.

The story is told of the disciple who, after several months, complained to his Master that he still had not been given a method or a technique. "What on earth would you want a method for?" asked the Master. "To attain to inner freedom," the disciple replied. The Master roared with laughter, saying: "You will need great skill indeed to set yourself free by means of the trap called a method!"

> What is more simple than prayer? Its spontaneity is sometimes lost by the use of methods that are too complicated. They may be useful to beginners but they are apt to provoke an excessive reaction in many souls. The latter, wearied by this complexity, sometimes sink into pious reverie without any real profit.
>
> — *Reginald Garrigou-LaGrange*[3]

The problem with methods — particularly more modern ones — is that they become a crutch, and instead of freeing us, they captivate us, holding us prisoners within the walls of their structures and techniques. Instead of being freed to come face to face with the Divine Presence, we continue to deal with the methods. Merton even warns that our meditation *postures* can subtly deceive us: "Look out for the external forms. It is so easy to take the external forms for the reality."[4] Conscious of our "prayer posture," we can easily convince ourselves that since we are in a *posture* of prayer, we are in fact truly praying.

Karl Rahner reminds us that "prayer is not a grand oratorio in a great cathedral but a simple folk-song in the chapel of our hearts." The counsel of St. Alphonsus de Ligouri is likewise apt:

Acquire the habit of speaking to God as if you were alone
with Him, familiarly and with confidence and love, as to the
dearest and most loving of friends.[5]

We must pray in the spirit of the publican and like the beg-
gar at the pool of Siloam, waiting for the "stirring of the
waters," the waters of grace. Over time our prayer should
become increasingly simplified. As is the case of two people
who experience the deepening of their love, words become
less and loving silence more. Thus the Spirit increasingly inspires and animates our prayer, teaching us the "language"
of God, which, as Eckhart reminds us, is silence. "Everything
else," adds Thomas Keating, "is a bad translation."

Lectio divina, the prayerful, meditative reading of Scripture, is always fruitful and must continue to nourish us
throughout our spiritual journey. As our prayer deepens, so
does our understanding of Scripture — depths beyond depths
beyond depths. The Holy Spirit "encounters herself" in the
words of Scripture, which she herself inspired. We must open
the pages of Scripture in an attitude of humble prayerfulness.

Do not approach the words of the mysteries contained in
the Scriptures without prayer, and asking for God's help.
Consider prayer to be the key to the understanding of truth in
Scripture.

— *St. Isaac the Syrian*[6]

St. Bonaventure teaches that persistent prayer can "bend
God's will" and *impel* God to grant us the gift of contemplation. In actual fact, God already desires this gift for us. It is
the bending of *our* will to his that God awaits, the distancing
ourselves from the allurements of the world. Humble, heartfelt prayer procures the graces that can dissolve the sludge
and dross of our lives. Like the blacksmith's iron that is able
to be bent after it has been subjected to fire, so our stub-
born will is gradually reshaped to conform to God's in the
purifying fire of the first dark night of the senses.

If we are faithful to our prayer discipline and endeavor to live it, this gifted night awaits us; it will transport us over the threshold that distinguishes the common from the mystical life, from spiritual childhood to spiritual adulthood. We don't like to think of ourselves as beginners. The humility to accept, with thanksgiving, that we can pray at all is a first step on the road of prayer. Though we may someday attain to the heights of mystical prayer, Merton reminds us, "we will still always be beginners."

> Believe me — and do not let anyone deceive you by showing you a road other than that of prayer.
>
> — *Teresa of Avila*[7]

11

A Time, a Place Apart

❦

Anyone who wants to get close to God must set aside a short time each day to speak to Him alone, a time of intimacy and encounter with the Lord. The actual place is of little importance, provided the soul finds there sufficient peace and silence.

— *Yves Raguin, S.J.*

It may not always be easy to find a quiet, secluded place where the noise and activity of the world will not intrude. Sometimes this requires considerable experimentation, particularly if we are a member of a large, bustling family or perhaps share a tiny apartment with another. Privacy is becoming more and more a scarcity — not simply the privacy of physical solitude but the privacy of quietude. The world is becoming increasingly noisy. We can no longer even go into a supermarket without being "caressed" by inane music and in-store commercials. Our Lord went up into the mountains to get away from the hustle and bustle of the world around him, a world considerably less frantic and turbulent than our own. If you are fortunate, there is a room in your home where, during certain times of the day or evening, the world can be barred from entering. If not, perhaps your "mountain" is the shadows of a darkened church, or a hushed meadow, or the corner of a nearby park.

Many years ago I had a long train commute to work. While the *New York Times* and the *Daily News* were raised like bleached stalks of wheat in the seats around me, I dis-covered my own little space could be made into something of a "hermitage." I could close my eyes undisturbed know-ing I did not have to get off the train until it dead-ended in Grand Central Station. I found the rhythmic, monotonous sound of the train's wheels to be conducive to "centering" and shutting out extraneous noises.

We are not monastics whose lives are carefully regulated to guarantee us time for private prayer and solitude. None-theless, there are always certain parts of the day or night when, if we cast about, the Lord will show us where we can carve out time for him alone. He will accommodate himself to our situation and never demand of us something that is beyond our means. Is it possible to go to bed a little earlier and rise a half hour or so earlier? Perhaps you are one of those who really don't "wake up" until later in the day. Af-ter others have retired and the house is still, perhaps this is your "prime time" for the Lord. To be sure, it is important to give the Lord, not our *spare* time but our *prime* time, when we are most alert and "with it." If we were dating someone, we would make sure we were always at our best in their com-pany, as bright-eyed as we could manage! There will be times, through no fault of ours, when we will be forced to fight sleep during prayer, though this should not be a steady occurrence. If it is, we should try to set aside another time of day or night or perhaps try to get an extra hour of sleep.

What about people who, in order to feed their family and keep their children in school, must work more than one job, laboring from the morning's early hours to late night, wind-ing up exhausted? One day a woman with many children and endless household chores came for advice to Teresa of Avila, disturbed that she could not find time to pray. Always the commonsense person, Teresa advised the woman to say short prayers throughout the day, during and between her many duties and chores. Sometimes we may have to wait until the burdens and complications of life grow lighter before we will have extended periods of time for prayer and quiet reflection.

At the time of his choosing, God will establish those open spaces in our life when we can be quietly alone with him.

It is no secret how Christian contemplative spirituality is "birthed" within us. The Word is eternally "spoken" by the Father in ineffable silence. The Spirit, the *ruah*, the breath of God, communicates the Word in silence to our own spirit, "pouring out the Spirit of the Son into our hearts" (Gal 4:6). To receive the Spirit in fullness we must dispose ourselves in *silent, receptive passivity.* The Spirit does not come on peals of thunder but on the soft silent clouds of inner peace and recollection.

> There should be at least a room or some corner where no one will find you and disturb you or notice you. You should be able to untether yourself from the world and set yourself free, loosing all the fine strings and strands of tension that bind you, by sight, by sound, by thought, to the presence of other men.
>
> — *Thomas Merton*[1]

12

The Monkey Mind

❧❦❧

> The mind is like a great tree inhabited by monkeys, swinging from branch to branch in an incessant riot of chatter and movement.
>
> — *Sri Ramakrisna*

The words of this renowned nineteenth-century Hindu mystic came home to me while on a photo-safari some years ago in Africa. There was a great tree just outside the walls of our campground inhabited by scores of monkeys. Left to themselves, the monkeys were fairly quiet, content to live peacefully in the tree and on the branches of their choice. However, whenever I approached the tree to get a closer look, the monkeys sent up a corporate howl, their high-pitched screeching revealing their indignation at my presence. The tree shook as monkeys by the dozens leapt from branch to branch, shrieking their displeasure. As soon as I returned to the campground, the monkeys settled down and all became peaceful once again.

Likewise, when we approach the fruitful tree of silent, wordless prayer, the "monkeys of our mind" cut loose, creating all kinds of annoying chatter, clatter, and images. These unwelcome thoughts are occasioned mostly by our daily activities and involvements and must neither be forcibly resisted or willfully entertained, but simply ignored. In the words of Teresa of Avila, "We should take no more notice of them than we would of an idiot."[1] Teresa compares such dis-

73

tractions to a madman running about in one's house. Should we chase after him (which is useless), we leave the Divine Guest unattended and alone. Bad manners to be sure!

While we had been meditating and praying discursively, the memory, the imagination, and the rational mind were engaged and more or less occupied. In wordless prayer we hand these lower faculties a "pink slip," informing them that their services are no longer needed. They rebel and immediately begin to "entertain us" with an ongoing "theater of the absurd" on the screen of our mind — coming attractions, cartoons, newsreels, short subjects and perhaps a "feature presentation." Our plans for the day, the things we must take care of, the letters we need to write, the distasteful experience we had with someone yesterday, or months before — all these "monkeyshines" surface endlessly. Until we learn to simply ignore their antics, they can cause consternation and anguish. In the end, they can even convince us that contemplative praying is not for us.

How we respond will determine whether or not we progress in prayer and advance along the spiritual journey. As soon as we learn to allow our stream of consciousness to simply amble on through and out of our mind and remain at peace during this surface commotion, our time will be well spent and extremely fruitful. We will make rapid progress both in prayer and in virtue, which are inexorably bound together. It is our sincere *intention* to be in God's presence at the time of our prayer that is important and at the heart of all contemplative prayer practices.

> When we have the impression that we have spent our time in prayer driving away distractions; when we have been left with our poverty with nothing but this striving for God, we can be sure that God has been acting in the depths of our soul. We perceive it afterward when we resume our other activities, by a sense of peace and rejuvenation in the depths of our heart.
> — *Thomas Philippe*[2]

As John of the Cross and others teach, it is only by faith that we access God. Prayer is the preeminent work of faith and therefore, like faith, often demands detachment from and the letting go of our feelings and emotions. "We must stand," Merton wrote, "naked and defenseless before God." This is the narrow way, the dark way, that leads to Life. By our faith, Christ is "released" to work deep within us. It is in times of darkness that he works most deeply within our "heart of hearts" to gradually transform us. Only our faith can assure us of this truth. Our deepest true self is much more than our feelings, our emotions, our thoughts, our psychological self. This is why it is our *intent* to pray, our *will* to pray that is essential in our prayer, a prayer rooted and grounded in faith.

If the refreshing dew of consolations has passed and the "dry season" has descended upon our land, we come face to face with the first decisive crisis of our journey. It is precisely at this juncture — calling for a blind leap of faith and trust — that most pray-ers throw up their hands and decide prayer is not for them — certainly not *this* kind of prayer! This is an alien country too foreboding and unfriendly for human habitation:

> The prospect of this wilderness is something that so appalls most people that they refuse to enter upon its burning sands and travel among its rocks. They cannot believe that contemplation and sanctity are to be found in a desolation where there is no food and no shelter and no refreshment for their imagination and intellect and the desires of their nature.
> — *Thomas Merton*[3]

We have stepped onto the narrow path that leads to life (it is narrower than first we think!), the path of naked faith and blind trust that leads to the in-breaking of the Kingdom of God within us, the bursting of the walls of separation, the healing of our divided consciousness. This is the way of the

Spirit, and "whoever are impelled by the Spirit are the true children of God" (Rom 8:14).

To repeat, it is our *intent* to be present and open to the Lord that is decisive. If our intent (the will) is sincere, then our prayer will *always* be fruitful and efficacious, even though we may have the "feeling" that our time has been spent doing nothing but dealing with distractions. Working unseen and "hiddenly," the Spirit breathes upon our secret heart, far beyond our ability to perceive, removed from our inquisitive scrutiny and observation. Sometimes during our time of prayer it may be a matter of simply enduring.

One of the great teachers of prayer, St. Jane Chantal, disciple of Francis de Sales, writes:

> In prayer, more is accomplished by listening than by talking. Let us leave to God the decision as to what shall be said. God speaks to the heart only when the heart is recollected.[4]

Grounded in faith, our apparently "useless" prayer is never such. In silence and in secret the Spirit heals us, enlarging our capacity for love, stripping away the ego-centered false self, renewing in us the image of the Son in whom we are created.

"If you never had any distractions," Merton writes, "then you don't know how to pray." When dryness and emptiness and the inability to pray or meditate as before come upon us, we should know that this darkness is the Spirit hovering over us, blinding our intellectual faculties and numbing our sense perceptions. God is Spirit and must work "spiritually." This "holy ignorance" is God detaching us from our prideful self-confidence and deep-rooted self assurance, stripping us of our dogged control. Only in the silent depths of our heart can the Spirit "blow inwardly" as she wills. In short, God is removing the greatest obstacle to His work in us — ourselves. Meister Eckhart said it succinctly: "Get out of the way and let God be God in you!"

Modern man needs to turn into his heart and, in silence, he must enter deeply into himself and hear his true Self, the Absolute Ground of all being tell him through experiential knowledge that the world of senses is not the totality of reality, but that through an experience man understands that he is one with all being. Modern man finds his greatest struggle in becoming silent before God's silent love.

— George A. Maloney[5]

13

Pure Prayer

❦

> When you pray, go into your chamber and bolt the door, and there pray to your Father in secret. And your Father in secret will reward you.
>
> *— John 6:6*

This Gospel passage makes unmistakable the need for a certain amount of silence and solitude in our lives if we are to pray well, if we are to grow. Without the deep cleansing waters of silence and solitude our spiritual life will be stunted and unfruitful, our spiritual arteries clogged. Though we may have left the fleshpots of Egypt, we will not cross its borders and enter the Promised Land of contemplation unless silence and solitude part the churning sea of activity that threatens to engulf us. Jesus enjoins us not only to seek physical solitude but to dispose ourselves for an *interior* solitude that springs up only out of the rich soil of silence. If "God is dead," his demise in us is due to the fact we may have talked him to death! We Americans, and Westerners in general, are verbalizing animals. We know little of interior silence, the womb of new and vital birth. A Buddhist saying strikes a profound note of truth: "The mind is the slayer of the soul." The great Eastern Father St. Isaac the Syrian urges: "More than all things love silence, for it will bring forth a fruit no tongue can describe."

"Do not babble on...do not use many words," Jesus teaches. We must, then, after we have offered our "few words," become attentively silent in an attitude of open, active receptivity. If we are not to "babble on," then we are clearly counseled *to be silent during the time remaining us.* This is how the Fathers of the Desert understood the counsel of Christ. They called this wordless, imageless prayer "pure prayer," or "prayer of the heart."

> Happy is the spirit who attains to perfect formlessness at the time of prayer. Do not by any means strive to fashion some image at the time of prayer.
>
> — *Evagrius Ponticus*[1]

When we go beyond the literal sense of the Gospel and search out what the Fathers called its mystical or hidden meaning, we see that when Jesus counsels us to "pray in secret," he intends more than simply isolating ourselves physically from observation and intrusion (bolting the door). The Lord invites us to a deeper, "pure prayer" that is existentially secret — secret not just to others but secret to ourselves.

In this silent, wordless, formless prayer "we do not know how to pray as we ought" (Rom 8:26). The "content" of our prayer is concealed from our understanding and our investigating mind. Having now "bolted the door" of our mind against words and images (but not distractions!), the Spirit is free to pray in us, which the Spirit will do if we allow her. This hidden prayer of the Spirit is impregnated with praise and thanksgiving. (The Desert Fathers considered thanksgiving the highest form of prayer). St. Gregory the Great counsels: "It is not by visible images and forms that one can obtain the divine light."

> He may well be loved, but He may not be thought. He may be reached and held close by means of love, but never by means of thought.
>
> — *The Cloud of Unknowing*[2]

The Advocate Jesus promised to send to help us pleads for us before the Father with "sighs too deep for words," praying in us "according to the mind of God" (Rom 8:26). The word "advocate" derives from the Greek judicial vocabulary, akin to "attorney" or "public defender." The Advocate, the Holy Spirit, "pleads our case" before the tribunal of God. At the same time, the Advocate will "teach us all things" (Jn 14:26) and teach us more in a few moments of silent, wordless prayer than in months, perhaps years, of discursive meditation and prayer.

To be silent and receptive before God is to be gradually awakened to a new and profound knowledge — to *experience* the loving knowledge of God in our hearts, the birthing and dilation of the Son who "increases in wisdom and stature and favor with God" (Lk 2:52). To know another person is to experience the reality of that person in our heart. In the religious experience, it is called "contemplation." To deeply know another person, we must be silent and open to that person's presence. To experience God, we must do likewise.

> Be still — and *know* that I am God.
>   — *Psalm 46:10*

14

Silence Whole and Healing

The present state of the world and all of life is diseased. If I were a doctor and were asked for my advice, I should reply: Create silence! Bring men to silence. The Word of God cannot be heard in the noisy world of today. And even if it were blazoned forth with all the panoply of noise so that it could be heard in the midst of all other noise, then it would no longer be the Word of God.

— *Søren Kierkegaard*

The world has become noise, silence its orphan child. The contemplative is a seed of silence planted amidst the jungle of noise, one whose harvest will come at a later time, perhaps a later age. The contemplative is a witness to silence, affirming that all things come out of silence and must return to silence to be healed and re-created.[1]

Every object has a hidden fund of reality that comes from a deeper source than the word that designates the object. Man can meet this hidden fund of reality only in silence. With his silence, man comes into relationship with the reality in the object which is there even before language ever gives it a name. This hidden fund of reality cannot be taken up into human language.

— *Max Picard*[2]

The silence of the contemplative does not attract attention. No one notices because the last thing a contemplative would want to be is noticed, still less, admired or thought of as "holy" (the contemplative is keenly aware of his or her own brokenness). The contemplative says what needs to be said and little else. Meaningless conversation is not only boring to the contemplative, but sometimes painful. This has nothing to do with snobbery or being antisocial, but with the need to be attentive to the indwelling Divine Guest, the source of the contemplative's silence who is constantly "tugging at the heart" for attention.

Much of our modern-day music proclaims the inner emptiness and "angst" of society. Raucous music, accompanied by mindless, orgiastic contortions in the guise of "expressing oneself" is transparent evidence of society's diseased cultural and spiritual state. Nothing is held back, nothing is sacred, nothing authentic is held in reserve. Such music is symptomatic of a world in upheaval. In the words of the Nigerian poet Ben Okai, "when chaos is the god of an era, clamorous music is the deity's chief instrument."

Heidegger observed that speech in our time has more and more degenerated into chatter. Meaningful conversation has become chit-chat, often riddled through and through with the intent to impresss and make oneself appear important. Silence is most often shattered not because of something that needs to be said (necessity preserves the spirit of silence) but, as Merton insightfully observed, *because of our need to be heard!* Language is a projection of the mind; silence is birthed from the womb of love. Silence is the home of the contemplative, even in the swirling midst of the world where he or she still remains a solitary. Hell, for a contemplative, is having to go to a cocktail party!

Everyone who delights in a multitude of words, even though he says admirable things, is empty within. If you love truth, be a lover of silence. Silence will unite you to God Himself. Love silence above everything else, for it brings a fruit the tongue is too feeble to describe. At first we must force ourselves to be silent, but then out of our silence is born something that

draws us into silence. May God grant you to perceive that
which is born of silence. If only you practice this, untold light
will dawn on you in consequence.

— *St. Isaac of Syria*[3]

"Nothing is so like God as silence," wrote Meister Eckhart. Silence is one thing (although it is not a "thing") that
has no value in modern life because it serves no utilitarian
function. Silence won't make anyone rich or successful.

Silence stands outside the world of profit and utility; it cannot
be exploited for profit; you cannot get anything out of it. It
is "unproductive." Therefore, it is regarded as valueless. Yet
there is more help and healing in silence than in all useful
things. It makes them whole again by taking them back from
the world of dissipation into the world of wholeness. The
mark of the Divine in things is preserved by their connection
with the world of silence.

— *Max Picard*[4]

"Man does not put silence to the test," Picard observes,
"silence puts *man* to the test." In silent prayer we are put to
the test of our willingness to sacrifice our exterior psychological self on the altar of a greater love. When we surrender our
dogged control by becoming silent, we allow the Holy Spirit
to pray in us and *become our prayer*. The Spirit gathers us
up, whole and entire, raising us as incense to the Father, from
whom the one Word, in silence, is eternally uttered. Nothing substantial is left behind, nothing overlooked, nothing
neglected.

Every good aspiration, every pressing need, all our weaknesses and the dark areas of our sinfulness are presented
whole and entire to the Father in the Son, whose members we
are. Every person we wish to remember, everyone for whom
we wish to pray or for whom we have been asked to pray, all
are enfolded in this Prayer of the Spirit who intercedes for

us with "unutterable groanings," with "sighs too deep for words" (Rom 8:26).

We need not tick off a laundry list of names of those we wish to place before God, nor enumerate one by one our needs and aspirations. The silence and emptiness of this prayer is holy, whole, and perfect, being of the Spirit who prays within us "according to the mind of God" (Rom 8:27). (The holistic "heart theology" of the fourth-century Syrian Church Father Pseudo-Macarius, which we will briefly consider in a subsequent chapter, is worth meditating upon in this context.)

> We must ask only for what God wants to give us. If we sense that our request is not pleasing to God, we must abandon it. As we become more and more contemplative, this prayer will simplify until finally the best petition will be little more than our simple presence. This also shows how to deal with the intentions that others recommend to our prayers. It is enough to take them deeply to heart at the moment they are entrusted to us. After that, our simply being present to God will constitute a petition.
>
> — *Thomas Philippe*[5]

Since, as Paul exclaims, "the Spirit of Jesus has been given us" (Gal 4:6), this same Spirit, living in our core-center, ranges the breadth and depth of our being. From this fathomless center, rooted in God, the Divine Therapist heals our festering wounds and begins to close the fissures and fault lines of our hurts, ills, and memories. No psychiatrist — not the greatest transpersonal psychiatrist — can reach so deep, for this center is beyond human observation and therefore beyond diagnosis and treatment. This is not to suggest for one moment that psychiatry has no role to play in our lives, spiritual or otherwise. Sometimes it may be not only necessary but even life-saving. Spare us from those who claim "all we need is Jesus." Psychiatry is a gift of God given us in modern times to help us with problems and stresses largely unknown in previous eras.

Rather, we are thinking of the so-called well-adjusted person within whom seethes an unsuspected cauldron that Jung calls the "shadow," containing the potential explosive power of a small atomic bomb, for good or for our self-destruction. Under the power of the Spirit, this energy is released and directed, enabling our noblest aspirations and our latent creativity to be realized.[6]

To "pray in the Spirit" is not the same as Prayer *of* the Spirit in the sense spoken of here. We can pray in the Spirit with words, song, and dance, and in tongues. Prayer of the Spirit is silent, secret (to ourselves), and wholly perfect and pleasing to the Father, "being of the mind of God." When we are struck dumb and do not know how to pray, when, like Job our tongue cleaves to the roof of our mouth, the Spirit will pray in us if we open ourselves in simple silent trusting faith.

> By whatever we call him, God's ultimate name can only be uttered, finally, in loving silence before his incomprehensibility.
>
> — *Karl Rahner*[7]

When we enter the "cave of our heart" and become silent before our silent God, "God speaks to God" on our behalf. In this receptive silence, we, God — all is at-oneness. We are being re-created, loved more and more into fuller being. As our union with God deepens, we become more our true selves, experiencing Teilhard de Chardin's insight that "love differentiates as it unites."

As we advance along the path of contemplative spirituality, an abyss begins to open up inside us and we hang precariously, so it seems, over a precipice, sometimes wondering if we are not hopelessly lost and abandoned and most to be pitied. It takes great faith and spiritual courage to stay the course of this silent, empty prayer, this surrender to darkness, aridity, and apparent nothingness. Once having stepped onto this narrowest of paths that leads to life, many refuse to tread it, for nothing is so inimical to their understanding of the spiritual life as this barren "nowhere" whose only inhabitant is emptiness.

> They cannot believe that contemplation and sanctity are to be found in a desolation where there is no food and no shelter and no refreshment for their imagination and intellect and for the desires of their nature.
>
> — *Thomas Merton*[8]

In his posthumous work "Contemplative Prayer," Thomas Merton quotes the twentieth-century "apostle of prayer" Abbé Monchanin, who poetically describes this experience:

> Now is the hour of the garden and the night, the hour of silent offering and therefore the hour of hope. God alone, faceless, unknown, unfelt. Yet, undeniably God![9]

15

The Hour of Silent Offering

In order to enter into the holy and mysterious communion
with the Word of God dwelling within us, we must first have
the courage to become more and more silent. In a deep creative silence we meet God in a way that transcends all the
powers of intellect and language. We know God is intimately
with us and is infinitely beyond us. It is only through deep and
liberating silence that we can reconcile the polarities of this
mysterious paradox.

— *John Main, O.S.B.*

There is a teaching tradition, specifically stated by John of
the Cross and Teresa of Avila, that one should not attempt
silent, wordless prayer until we are certain we have been
called to it (in the dark night of sense). Much has been
learned, however, since the sixteenth century from develop-
mental psychology and from contact with the meditation
practices of the East. We have learned of the four Jungian
basic personality types, further subdivided into sixteen by
Myers-Briggs. We now understand there are certain types of
intuitive, reflective people who are naturally and easily disposed simply to "be" in silence, who would find praying
with words and images difficult and uncomfortable. For such
people, discursive prayer can become an obstacle. (Teresa of
Avila and Thérèse of Lisieux experienced great difficulty with
discursive prayer and gave up the attempt. St. Thérèse could
not pray the Rosary, which, for her, was a hindrance).

Today there is a reaction against discursive prayer. Yet, this
is a good solid form of prayer. Many people have begun with
discursive prayer and ended up consummate mystics. The
path traced out by mystical theologians — discursive prayer
to infused contemplation — is very valuable, *provided we
do not consider it a road everyone must travel.* Mystical
contemplation is not extraordinary. It is very ordinary. All
Christians, I believe, are called to it, and when they follow this
path they become their true selves [emphasis added].
— *William Johnson*[1]

The great spiritual paths of the East vault over preparatory discursive meditation largely by use of the mantra, the
repetition of a sacred sanskrit word or phrase that works to
prevent the stream of consciousness from asserting itself and
catching up the meditator on a particular thought or distraction. In the East, the seeker is given the practice of a mantra
at the very outset of his or her spiritual journey.

The mantra is a powerful tool for quieting the mind during the
process of meditation. Not only can you use the mantra for
the formal practice of meditation, but it also can be repeated
silently as you go about your daily activities.
— *Swami Muktananda*[2]

This conforms closely with the teaching of John Cassian
in his famous Conferences on Prayer, a path taught him
by the holy Desert Father Abba Isaac.[3] The Desert Fathers,
realizing a simple structure was needed to support their striving for continuous prayer, would select a short phrase from
Scripture and gently repeat it as they went about their daily
chores. Others took up the Jesus Prayer, sometimes called the
great Christian mantra, or simply the name of Jesus, weaving
this simplest of prayers into their daily activities. In time, they
were gifted with the simple habitual presence of God in their
hearts, in which they "rested," having been transformed into

"living prayers" by the Holy Spirit. In time, the mantra "falls away," leaving only a simple gifted Presence.

Until he died recently, Daniel O'Hanlon was Professor of Theology at the Jesuit School of Theology at Berkeley, California. He writes: "I made a new discovery through my contact with Asian practices. I found that one can move toward the goal of prayer beyond words and concepts without necessarily beginning with words and concepts." Noting that he had traveled extensively in India and the principal Buddhist countries seeking to deepen his own Christian spiritual life, Fr. O'Hanlon met many thousands of young people on the same trail. For himself his search was "not because I was disillusioned with my own Christian faith; I was seeking to enrich it." He writes:

> One of the discoveries I made over and over again from lengthy interviews with many young people searching for deeper religious experience was their inability to find teachers in the West who could guide them. At the same time they repeatedly revealed their almost total ignorance of the historical existence of a vigorous Christian contemplative tradition.[4]

At some point along our prayer path, we must slow down and halt the interior dialogue. Whether we realize it or not (mostly not) we are constantly talking to ourselves, an interior dialogue that mutters on and on from our rising to our falling asleep at night. Quieting this internal dialogue is essential in all contemplative prayer practices, be it by use of a mantra or, as in Centering Prayer, bringing a one- or two-syllable word internally into play, as *The Cloud of Unknowing* teaches, whenever we become conscious of being caught up in a distraction.

Most intellectuals and hyperactive people will encounter great difficulty if they attempt to begin with silent, wordless prayer. "Yet," as Thomas Keating observes, "if you could get them to do that, all of the things they do will become better as soon as they start."[5] Our Western culture and methods of recent centuries have conditioned us to believe we must be "doing something" in prayer in order to properly pray. We have become convinced it is the only way to pray. We have thus become trapped in a flawed conviction. "Touching the place of silence and experiencing the presence of God," Thomas Keating writes, "will prevent us from getting stuck on one of the preparatory levels."[6]

> Traditional prayer forms no longer seem to help us Christians to meet the living God of Abraham, Isaac, and Jacob. Western Christianity has based its prayer forms largely on an exhausted scholastic philosophy and theology concerning human beings, God and the material world. A spiritual vision is needed that can break through this Augustinian Platonism, which has accounted so often for an un-Christian separation of God and His creation.
>
> — *George A. Maloney, S.J.*[7]

This spiritual vision of which George Maloney writes is found in the contemplative prayer practices of the early Eastern Church and the Desert Fathers of fourth-century Egypt, Syria, and Palestine called "prayer of the heart."[8]

Our God is a silent God who is not interested in the appearances of words and images (which can be called "spiritual materialism") but who looks hard at our heart, the deepest depth of our true inner self:

> God does not see as man sees. Man sees only appearances, but God looks into the heart.
>
> — *1 Samuel 16:7*

Accepting our silent sacrifice, the Father "in secret rewards us" by ever so gently and gradually healing our brokenness through the power of the Spirit of Jesus within us. In this silence, we offer God our true selves and not the bogus "straw man" of the false exterior self, a self capable of projecting only words and images. In this silence, we offer God the only gift we have of value, the gift of our inner need, poverty, and destitution — the priceless gift of our brokenness.

> My sacrifice is this broken spirit. You will not scorn this crushed and broken heart.
>
> *— Psalm 51:17*

16

The Garden of the Night

⚜

In the same way that God is darkness to the mind, faith enlightens our understanding by blinding it. Only by this means
does God manifest Himself to the soul in a divine light which
exceeds all understanding. Whence it results that the greater
the faith, the more profound is the union, for under the darkness of faith the understanding is united to God; under cover
of this mysterious darkness, God is found hidden.

— *John of the Cross*

Those who initially may be led by the way of discursive
prayer should, at some point, begin to hunger for something
deeper, something more satisfying than the poverty of their
own words, thoughts, and ideas. Like certain animals who
sense water beneath the ground and dig for it until they find
it, some will sense there is an underground river that, if they
find it, will slake their thirst. The inner self is beginning to cry
out for the living waters that alone can satisfy it, water that
runs pure and silent and deep and that can become a fountain
of water inside us, welling up into new life.

A poignant story is recounted of the elderly Egyptian Desert Father Paphnutius who, over the many years of his long
life, envisioned God in human form, having taken literally
the words of Genesis: "Let us make man in our own image
and likeness." When a learned visitor came to his monastery,
the visitor took great pains to explain that God is formless
and immaterial. Upon hearing this, the old man threw him-

self down on the ground, giving way to sobs and tears, and exclaiming: "They have taken my God away from me. I have no one to hold on to and I do not know whom to address or adore!"[1] Like the devout Paphnutius we too must learn to cut through our "spiritual materialism" by shedding words and images and finding the immaterial formless God in naked faith, heeding the counsel of Meister Eckhart: "In order to find God, we must let go of God."

For many, there is no need to make a conscious decision to enter into wordless, imageless prayer. The Spirit makes the decision for us, leading us into the first of the passive purifications, the night of sense. In this dark fire the Spirit dries up our facility for words and thoughts and defeats our once facile ability to meditate. Not understanding at first what is happening, we experience terrible loss, the loss of the very God we were seeking and *thought we had found* (for our *feelings* told us so!). This, however, was not the God of Abraham, Isaac, and Jacob, but the God of our own imaginings and projections, not the "I Am" of the Almighty, but the God of our own subjective construct. We come face to face with the painful knowledge that we do not know who or what God is.

> God leaves them in such darkness that they do not know which way to turn in their discursive imaginings; they cannot advance a step in meditation, as they used to, now that the interior sensory faculties are engulfed in this night. He leaves them in such dryness that they not only fail to receive satisfaction and pleasure from their spiritual exercises and works, as they did formerly, but also find these exercises distasteful and bitter.
>
> *— John of the Cross*[2]

We are being schooled, in St. Bernard's words, in "learned ignorance" that will teach us a new and higher knowledge beyond our intellectual capacities. This new light "shines in darkness," a light our darkness cannot comprehend (Jn 1:5).

If we are faithful and docile to this "dark light," we will come to experience what the great mystics have variously called "luminous obscurity," or "bright darkness" or "seeing without seeing." We will experience the words of Meister Eckhart: "There, above the mind, God shines!"

Those who remain trusting and at peace in this "cloud of unknowing" soon come to realize they are being led directly by God. If they continue faithful to their dark and arid prayer, they will make rapid progress and come to profound union with God, a union in which they already now share a most precious portion. They will be taught directly by God and will be "anointed in the truth" (1 Jn 2:27). Yahweh will "lead them into the wilderness and, there, will speak to their hearts" (Hos 2:14).

Welcome, friend, to the garden of the night, the hour of hope and not despair. Here, within the shadowed cloister of this garden, you will find the living waters for which you thirst. You are being tried as gold in the furnace (1 Pet 1:7), being pruned that you may bear fruit aplenty (Jn 15:2), called to oneness with Christ in God (Jn 17:13, 21). In this secret garden, in this eclipse of your rational faculties, you will flower and bloom and become a new creation. This strange and foreign land you will soon call "home." You will come to be at peace here and be profoundly grateful you are one of its citizens.

This peace will gradually seep deeper and deeper into your very soul. You will find that the darkness and the aridity and the accompanying trials and temptations will not upset or confuse you as once they did. But you must have invincible faith and trust and return, day after day, to your dark and arid prayer come what may. You are learning what it means to truly pray, to truly love:

Prayer and love are really learned in the hour when prayer has become impossible, and your heart turns to stone.

— *Thomas Merton*[3]

17

As Prometheus Chained

❦

I have come to cast fire upon the earth, and how I wish it were
already ablaze!

— Luke 12:49

There is an ancient tradition that has preserved a saying at-
tributed to Jesus, perhaps one of many lost to us in the
Gospel writings: "He who is near me is near fire." Most of
us prefer to remain close enough to the fire to soak up a little warmth from time to time, but prefer to remain too far
removed to be enkindled. Nonetheless, we must enter this
fire to be re-created, to "put on the new self created in God's
way" (Eph 4:24). We stay mostly at "arm's length" from the
fire by praying with words, words, words. We must willingly
enter into it with both feet, freed from the shackles of words
and images. Every word we utter is, by its very definition,
limited and circumscribed.

Each word, therefore, is a "cage" that takes on meaning as
we connect up other "cages" to convey thoughts and ideas.
When we talk to God, we link up innumerable "cages" and
construct a lovely, perhaps even elegant, cage of words and
images. *How beautiful is the prison we have built for the
Wild Lord of the Cosmos!* We can congratulate ourselves for
succeeding to cage a God too unpredictable and too threat-
ening for us to otherwise manage. For this is a dangerous
and jealous God who wishes to invade every atom of our
being and burn away the false exterior self with which we

95

have become so comfortable and familiar. "Looking in" from outside the cage, we admire God's perfections and attributes, every one of which is but a projection of our own imagining. Everything we assert about God, as Eckhart reminds us, we must deny, for our puny conceptions fall infinitely short of God's reality. In Hindu terms, God is "not this, not that." In Christian terms, God is only "I Am." The "suchness" of the Father is known only to the Son, who is in "the bosom of the Father," in the mutuality and fecundity of the Holy Spirit.

The Father of Western apophatic mysticism, Pseudo-Dionysius, writes: "We must not dare apply words or conceptions to this hidden God"[1] There is no greater false security than to believe we can "grasp God" by thoughts or concepts. Meanwhile, our infinitely humble God "paces the cages" we have so methodically fashioned for him, desiring only to be released into our hearts where his fire can heal us at our deepest depths. The God we conceive and project is the God we get — a God scaled down to our own littleness. *This is a God we make helpless to re-create us!*

The cages we build for God become our own prisons. We become like the fabled Prometheus of Greek mythology, who, because he was chained, could not steal fire from heaven. In silent, wordless, formless prayer we "steal fire from heaven" by means of the Spirit who now prays in us, fire that heals and cauterizes our deep wounds and fissures. Until this Spirit-fire both slakes and purifies us, we will never truly experience that we are children of God. In contemplative prayer, the Spirit gradually dislodges the "junk" of a lifetime, going back to earliest childhood, the hidden debris of hurts, angers, and resentments that obstruct the inflow of grace at our deepest depths.

Someone who has gone through the "spiritual Twelve Steps" is not yet healed, nor has that person achieved individuation according to Jung's concept. Such a person is now only *prepared* to receive the deeper healing of inner transformation. The Divine Therapist, renewing us at our inmost depths, initiates and accomplishes our healing over the many years, cutting between "the marrow and bones" (Heb 4:12), a surgical process that can be quite painful and discomforting. Better now than later. In the blinding reality of death, this transformation continues without our cooperation and without merit. The "love therapy" called purgatory completes our transformation.[2] It is a fire, to be sure, but a spiritual "love-fire" that completes the eradication of all self-centeredness and self-love.

We are enjoined, however, not to tarry and squander the infinitely precious gift of life, created for union with God, but to "go forth to meet the Bridegroom on his way" (Mt 25:1) carrying lamps filled with oil — the perfumed oil of our prayer and good works. Our "spiritual trajectory" when we depart this life will determine the fullness of the Vision that "eye has not seen nor ear heard" — an unthinkable adventure that, in the words of Gregory of Nyssa, eternally progresses from "glory to glory." Heaven, hell, or purgatory begin in this present life. We are free to choose.

> The Spirit and the Bride say, "Come." Let everyone listening say, "Come." All who desire it may have the water of life, and have it free.
>
> — *Revelation 22:17*

Part Three

Night-Birth:
The Awakening Heart

18

God Said: Let There Be Darkness

ೲಊ

God now leaves them in such darkness that they do not know
which way to turn; they cannot advance a step in meditation
as they used to now that the sensory faculties are engulfed in
this night. He leaves them in such dryness that they fail not
only to receive satisfaction and pleasure from their spiritual exercises and works, but also find these exercises distasteful and
bitter. This usually happens to recollected beginners sooner
than to others.

— *John of the Cross*

When we first read of the dark nights in the writings of John
of the Cross they may sound dramatic, even romantic. There
is nothing dramatic or romantic about a crucifixion, especially when it is our own! This unexpected desolation is not
what we thought the spiritual journey was about.

Convinced that perfection is to be measured by brilliant
intuitions of God and fervent resolutions of a will on fire
with love, and persuaded that sanctity is a matter of sensible
favors and tangible results, they will have nothing to do with
a contemplation that does not delight their reason and invest
their minds and wills with consolations and sensible joys.

— *Thomas Merton*[1]

St. Gregory of Nyssa, the fourth-century Father of apophatic mysticism (the *via negativa,* or dark path to God),

describes the spiritual journey as a passage from light to
darkness to light. Before the light we must first pass through
a dark fire that burns away the secret spiritual ambition and
yearnings of our sense appetites, a secret seeking of the *gifts*
of God rather than love of God for himself alone. If we are
more or less faithful and generous during this first purgation
of the senses, we will be gifted with the more profound and
terrible night of the spirit, which will purge the deeply rooted
defects and infirmities of the spirit. Though we were to put
on sackcloth and ashes, fast until our bones protruded, and
wear ourselves out with charitable works, we could not, of
ourselves, sufficiently attain to that purity of heart whereby
we are given to "see God."

> No matter how much an individual does through his own
> efforts, he cannot actively purify himself enough to be
> disposed in the least degree for the divine union of the
> perfection of love. God must take over and purge him in fire
> that is dark for him.
>
> *— John of the Cross*[2]

> In spite of all its generosity the soul cannot completely purify
> itself so that it will be even slightly fit for divine union in the
> perfection of love. God Himself must put His hand to work
> and purify the soul in this fire that is hidden from it.
>
> *— John of the Cross*[3]

Upon the ashes of our false ego self, God alone can fashion a
"new creation" that will attain to "the perfect knowledge of
God" (Eph 4:13). In the first night of sense, the Spirit broods
over us, casting us into great darkness:

> God leaves them in such darkness that they do not know
> which way to turn in their discursive imaginings. They cannot
> advance a step in meditation as they used to now that
> the interior sensory faculties are engulfed in this night. He
> leaves them in such dryness that they not only fail to receive

satisfaction and pleasure from their spiritual exercises and works, as they did formerly, but also find these exercises distasteful and bitter.

— John of the Cross[4]

The Carmelite saint ascribes these conditions to the time of prayer. Our intellectual faculties fully return to us during the activities of the day, keener and more acute than before. This desert night is God's invitation to union. It is God's voice crying out in the wilderness of our inmost self, calling us to holiness and wholeness. The Spirit is attending to a profound purification beyond our ability to perceive and observe — a "power working in us which can do infinitely more than we can ask or imagine" (Eph 3:20). It is the vital and radical purgation of our false, exterior self that is necessary if we are to bear fruit aplenty and truly become His disciples (Jn 15:2, 8).

The first sign of infused prayer is this inexplicable and undaunted seeking, this quest that is not put off by aridity or darkness or frustration. On the contrary, in deepest darkness the soul finds peace, and in suffering it does not lack joy. Pure faith and blind hope are enough. Clear knowledge is not necessary.

— Thomas Merton[5]

If we are faithful to our dark and "empty" prayer, in spite of the onslaught of distractions and aridity, we can be confident we are on the path that leads to the living waters of contemplation and Divine union. In Merton's words, "If we are faithful, it will be our destiny."

The man who does not permit his spirit to be beaten down and upset by dryness and helplessness, but who lets God lead him peacefully through the wilderness and desires no other support or guidance than that of pure faith and trust in God alone, will be brought to the Promised Land. He will taste the peace and joy of union with God. He will, without "seeing," have a habitual, comforting, obscure and mysterious awareness of his God present and acting in all the events of life.

— Thomas Merton[6]

19

Embrace the Night

❧

Souls that are submissive and accept their first trials enjoy
peace in a short time, and then the knowledge how to find
God in darkness. As a result of this knowledge, they make
rapid progress.

— *Reginald Garrigou-LaGrange*

With the night of sense we have entered upon precarious
ground. There is a painful perception that we are lost, that
God has abandoned us, that we have probably offended God,
though we cannot remember how. We are faced with two
choices: we can flee the darkness and return to former ways
of prayer and meditation (which may not always even be
possible), or we can take off our shoes and walk onto the
burning sands of this desert night, trusting in God to lead
and protect us.

"The experience of the contemplative," Merton writes, "is
not so much one of victory as of defeat." Defeated are the
clear ideas and reasonings of the intellect now no longer
able to function during prayer. Vanquished is the secret self-
assurance that former lights and consolations afforded us.
We are suddenly brought low. What we once thought we
knew of God and the things of God is now the faintest of
memories. We discover we are ignorant of God and blind to
God's light.

Although perceiving themselves lost and floundering, those
who find peace in this barren land somehow understand in

time that this is the way it is supposed to be. They intuit they are traveling in the right direction, albeit in no direction. Illumined by an intensification of the gifts of the Spirit, they sense this alien land is not an enemy, but a friend. Everything is turned inside out and upside down. The night seems unexplainably "brighter" than the daylight of clear concepts and ideas. This bitter desert is "sweeter" than the green pastures of yesterday. We are tempted to tenuously say: "Lord, it is good for us to be here" (Mt 17:4). Although we do not understand what is happening, we would defend this small parcel of desert with our lives!

> If those in whom this occurs know how to remain quiet, without care or solicitude about any interior or exterior work, they will soon in that unconcern and idleness delicately experience the interior nourishment. This refection is so delicate that if the soul tries to experience it, it cannot. This contemplation is active while the soul is in idleness and unconcern. It is like air that escapes when one tries to grasp it.
>
> *— John of the Cross*[1]

> Often the person so favored does not understand this love and has no feeling of it, since it is not established in the senses by tenderness, but in the soul by fortitude, courage and daring hitherto unknown to it.
>
> *— John of the Cross*[2]

During this night it is critical that we resist the temptation to "tinker" with God's secret, sanctifying work. We must not try to force interior pious acts or attempt to "squeeze out" drops of sensible consolation. To do so would seriously impede the divine action.

> In order to be supernaturally transformed, the soul...must remain in darkness, like a blind person, relying on obscure

faith, taking it as light and guide. The soul creates great
obstacles for itself when it relies on reasoning or is attached
to its own will.

— John of the Cross[3]

The Mystical Doctor goes on to explain something of the
mysterious hidden process by which God is transforming the
submissive soul:

In the same way that God is darkness for our mind, faith
enlightens our understanding by blinding it. Only by this
means does God manifest Himself to the soul in a divine light
which exceeds all [rational] understanding; whence it results
that the greater the faith, the more profound is the union,
for under the darkness of faith the understanding is united to
God; under cover of this mysterious darkness, God is found
hidden.[4]

The prayer of St. Paul on our behalf is being answered:

May He give you the power through His Spirit for your
hidden self to grow strong . . . until you are filled with the utter
fullness of God."

— Ephesians 3:14, 19

In this spiritual "college of hard knocks," the Divine Guru
will teach us everything and "bring us to the complete truth"
(Jn 16:13). In silence, in darkness, in aridity, and in emptiness, God is secretly infusing a loving knowledge of himself
and his Mysteries — a knowledge infinitely exceeding all
the knowledge in all the books in all the libraries in all the
world.

The soul understands that without the noise of words this
Divine Master is teaching it by suspending its faculties. For
if they were to work they would do harm rather than bring
benefit. The soul is being enkindled in love, and it doesn't

understand how it loves. It seems that this good cannot be merited or gained through all the trials one can suffer on earth. This good is a gift from the Lord of heaven and earth who gives according to Who He is.

— Teresa of Avila[5]

20

Gifts of the Night

❧❧❧

One dark night,
fired with love's urgent longings
— ah, the sheer grace! —
I went out unseen,
my house being now all stilled.
— *John of the Cross,*
"Stanzas of the Soul"

The Mystical Doctor explains the first stanza of his poem as depicting the departure of the soul from inordinate self-love and attachment to created things and spiritual consolations. As the dark night progresses in aridity, our taste and desire for *things* dries up, leaving us with a disinterestedness in worldly ways and allurements. Before, our efforts to distance and detach ourselves from their sticky influences were difficult. Now it is relatively easy. The gift of knowledge, which predominates during this purifying night, has revealed the emptiness and hollowness of created things. Things temporal and material become "neutral," often distasteful and sometimes even bitter — but mostly, just plain uninteresting. What once used to allure and captivate us now repels. Things and pleasures we once "had to have" now fade into the remote shadows of life. Our spiritual "taste buds" having been purified, our inordinate appetite for creaturely things is taken from us.

God so curbs concupiscence and bridles the appetite through
this arid and dark night that the soul cannot feast on any
sensory delight from earthly or heavenly things. He continues
this purgation in such a way that the concupiscence and the
appetites are brought into subjection, reformed and mortified.
                                          — *John of the Cross*[1]

Problems that once almost totally absorbed us no longer
usurp our time, for we have discovered that most of these
"problems" either take care of themselves or were never
really substantial problems to begin with. This is not to suggest that real and serious problems do not remain requiring
our care and thoughtful attention, but even genuine problems
are seen and dealt with differently, in the context of a greater
reality that surrounds, enfolds, and animates us.

This new climate in which we find ourselves is fostered by
a diminishment of our false ego-self. The gift of knowledge,
which revealed to us the emptiness of things, also penetrates
the disguise of the ego-I, revealing it for what it is — vacuous
and unsubstantial.

In the dryness and emptiness of this night of the appetite, a
person also procures spiritual humility, that virtue opposed
to the first capital vice, spiritual pride. Through this humility,
acquired by means of self-knowledge, a person is purged of
all those imperfections of the vice of pride into which he fell
in the time of his prosperity.
                                          — *John of the Cross*[2]

Emptiness and nakedness of spirit are gifts of this night
that define the essential experience and orientation of the
contemplative life. Our former sense of self-sufficiency, now
stripped away, leaves us with a void by which we come
to understand our nothingness. Confronted with our inner
poverty as creatures, we come to understand our utter de-
pendency on God, our deepest Self, our true life.

Once prancing about as the epitome of everything real and meaningful, the ego-I is being shorn of its costume and mask and exposed for its falsity — a skeleton of dry bones. Though still very much present, the ego — like a chameleon that senses danger — quickly changes colors, clothing itself in "spiritual colors." The ego now moves about in a much more subtle and difficult-to-detect skin, its most poisonous venom being secret spiritual pride. Another night still to come will be the ego's Waterloo.

Like a performer on stage followed by a pin-spot, the ego-I in its movements is detected and illuminated by the penetrating lamp of contemplation. Each time the ego makes a move to assert itself, this inner light "spots" it as it emerges from the wings onto center stage. Alert and awakened by the lamp of the Spirit, the deep inner self is now capable of detecting this "actor," which seeks to upstage it and assume the starring role. With a simple, prayerful inward glance of recognition, the inner self — like in the days of vaudeville — can "throw the hook" and whisk this grotesque imposter offstage. All of this is analogy and metaphor, but nonetheless quite real — though, like contemplation itself, it can be understood only by someone who has had experience of these delicate interior dynamics.

Of the different graces infused by the gift of knowledge the most prominent is the gifted knowledge of our own self. When people say they "know themselves" they are almost always speaking of their exterior or psychological self. True knowledge of self goes much deeper and can be revealed only by grace that unveils the inner landscape beneath the surface of our psychological exterior self.

This spiritual light reveals our inner poverty and destitution, the ruins of our interior house. Now conscious and aware of our own needfulness, we are no longer tempted to swiftly and harshly judge others (projections of the false self) for we now have *experiential evidence* of our own impoverished condition. If we accept and embrace the truth of our great need for healing (the real meaning of "salvation") we have taken the first giant step in our journey toward spiritual growth and maturity.

Shining out of the night of contemplation, a "ray of darkness" increasingly illumines our ruined house, bringing us face to face with what Merton calls "existential dread," a time of crisis and decision. This progressive unmasking of our inner destitution calls for a brutal honesty not only to recognize the poverty of our condition but to wholeheartedly accept and embrace it, a decision calling for great spiritual courage.

> During the dark night...anxiety is felt in prayer, often acutely. This is necessary because this spiritual night marks the transfer of the full, free control of our inner life into the hands of a superior power. This means too that the time of darkness is, in reality, a time of hazard and difficult options.
>
> If we set out into this darkness, we have to meet these inexorable forces. We will have to face fears and doubts...and, at this moment, precisely, all spiritual light is darkened, all values lose their shape and reality and we remain, so to speak, in the void.
>
> — *Thomas Merton*[3]

To be sure, we do not wish to deal with this unpleasant specter, often ignoring it as irrelevant. What is equally harmful is to *dwell* on this dark side and accord it too much attention and concern. When someone attempts to communicate this existential dread to a priest — as someone recently informed me — the priest might ask if that person has considered seeing a psychiatrist! It isn't the well-intentioned penitent that's going crazy; the problem lies with the confessor who has no experience or knowledge of the contemplative/mystical path and begins to tinker superficially with the spiritual state of the person who has come to him for help.

113

We must face the fact that Catholic seminaries do not prepare seminarians for the mystical life, nor do they offer the
theological grounding necessary to guide others through the
twists and turns of the dark path of the contemplative journey. Until there are more priests (and other religious) who
are mystics, this will continue to sap the spiritual vitality of
the Church. Otherwise, how will the priest be able to feed
the flock under his care? How will he be able to guide those
called to the mystical life who may come to him for help? As
a young man approaches the day of his ordination he should
be well along the path of the contemplative journey. The Vatican II Dogmatic Constitution on the Church proclaims that
all priests must "abound in contemplation" to the joy of the
people of God.[4] In our times especially, guides are needed
who are themselves mystics. Is it too radical to suggest that
ordination be denied those who have little or no desire for
the mystical life?

The intensification of grace during the night of sense
(which is darkness to our experience) radically cleanses us
of impediments that obstruct God's grace, preventing it from
taking root — or in the words of Macarius, from "pasturing
our hearts." This "pasturing of the heart" radiates throughout our entire being, birthing a *habitual consciousness* of the
indwelling God who gently, continually "haunts" us. This
simple, delicate, loving awareness of God is the gift of contemplation. Even at its nascent stage of development, there
is a sense we are participating in God's own life, a life that
all Christians are called to experience consciously. We repeat
here the declaration of Carl Jung: "It is pointless to praise
the Light if nobody can see it!"

> The soul bears an habitual remembrance of God, accompa-
> nied by a fear and dread of turning back on the spiritual road.
> This is a notable benefit... because the soul is purified of the
> imperfections which of themselves make it dull... and cling
> to it by means of appetites and affections.
>
> — *John of the Cross*[5]

It is no wonder that John of the Cross calls this the "*happy night of the senses*" — in spite of (rather, *because* of) its purifying darkness and aridity. In this first night we are given an unerring sense that, although we are in the world and much involved in it, we are, by grace, no longer *of* it — at least not nearly to the degree as before. LaGrange asserts: "The contemplative enjoys a *relative* perfection" (for those who might dwell on this, here is an unlocked entrance for spiritual pride!). However, there are still many miles to go and many crosses to bear, and the shadow of Golgotha looms up ahead. Like the One we follow, no one can take our life from us unless we *choose* to lay it down of our own free will, a choice distinguished by the marks of generosity and docility.

> I tell you most solemnly that unless the grain of wheat falls into the ground and dies it remains only a single grain; but if it dies, it yields a rich harvest. Anyone who loves their life will lose it; anyone who hates their life in this world will keep it for eternal life.
>
> *—John 12:24–25*

21

That Your Joy May Be Full

❧

In the dark night the soul is weaned from sensible consolations which at a certain time have their value, but which become an obstacle when they are sought for their own sake. Hence the necessity of the passive purification of the senses which establishes the soul in aridity and leads it to a spiritual life which is more detached from the senses, imagination and reasoning. By the gifts of the Holy Spirit, the soul at this time receives an intuitive knowledge which, despite a very painful darkness, initiates it profoundly into the things of God.

— *Reginald Garrigou-LaGrange*

Until the purgation of the night of sense is undergone, much self-love and pride stand between ourselves and loving union with God. Most of this self-love is hidden from us, for we do not have sufficient light to perceive it. The lamp of contemplation has not yet illuminated our deeply ingrained self-love and selfish motivations.

Dependence on sense feelings, a need for recognition, secret pride — all are at work in our activities and projects. The seven capital sins, as Thomas Keating reminds us, are quietly at work. These faults and infirmities must be purged if we are to attain to a new quality of living, the "way of contemplation" and the mystical life.

A *second conversion,* such as St. Peter ("a good and devout man") underwent following his denial of Christ and which the saints underwent, is vital. Thomas Merton, who had a remarkable ability to uncover the root causes of things, identifies the scarcity of second conversions to illusion and self-deception: "It is relatively easy to convert the sinner, *but the good are often completely unconvertible* simply because *they do not see the need for conversion*" (emphasis added).[1]

This insight of Merton's strikes at the heart of a certain malaise, a lack of fire, that permeates modern Christianity today. Countless Christians, called to union in the perfection of love, dutifully go to church on Sundays, say a few prayers during the week, and perhaps engage in their favorite devotional exercises. Yet the deep inner self remains aloof:

> So far as our spiritual life consists of thoughts, desires, actions, devotions and projects of our exterior self, it participates in the non-being and exterior falsity of that exterior self.
> — *Thomas Merton*[2]

The thought never occurs to them that their lives are in need of a second conversion. As long as this complacent attitude persists, Christianity will stay mired in a certain malaise. Fortunately, there are "pockets of fire" in the Church that continue to infuse vitality and passion into its life, mystics who, like randomly scattered fires, burn silently in the near and far-flung fields of Christianity. These pockets of fire, the "Church of the little flock" as Karl Rahner describes them, will, as he foresaw, rekindle the Church anew in a coming age. Such fires are holding everything together and keeping the world from coming apart at the seams.

> Mysticism is not confined to a privileged few. Mysticism is the truly dynamic element in the Church, which transcends the mere observances of the letter of the law and gives the sacramental and institutional Church the full richness of the inward spirit which promotes their efficacy.
> — *Karl Rahner*[3]

Thomas Merton emphasizes that conversion to Christ is not merely the conversion from bad habits to good habits, but becoming a *totally new person* in Christ.

In the first chapters of *The Dark Night,* John of the Cross writes in great detail of the faults of beginners, which can be reduced to three: spiritual pride, spiritual sensuality, and spiritual laziness (LaGrange). Vain curiosity, exaggerating our own worth (and wanting it to be recognized), judging others, a secret eagerness for self-seeking — these are some of the hidden faults of beginners enumerated by the Saint of Carmel:

> Beginners feel so fervent and diligent in their spiritual exercises and undertakings that a secret pride is generated in them. They desire to speak of spiritual things in other's presence, and sometimes even instruct rather than be instructed. In their hearts they condemn others who do not seem to have the kind of devotion they would like them to have.[4]

> Sometimes they minimize their faults and at other times are discouraged by them. Since they felt they were already saints, they become impatient and angry with themselves. They are often extremely anxious that God remove their faults and imperfections, but their motive is personal peace rather than God.[5]

No amount of mortification — or prayer — can heal these infirmities at their roots. They must be inwardly cleansed by God that a fitting abode be prepared for the new inflowing of the Holy Spirit who comes secretly in the first dark night. As we journey into this night, God establishes those virtues in the soul that only God can produce, which God does imperceptibly in a "dark fire." Concurrently, the Spirit deepens and vivifies the theological virtues of faith, hope, and charity, virtues infused directly by God whose full development is proper only to the mystical life.

> The attainment of supernatural transformation manifestly
> demands a darkening of the soul and an elevation above all
> sensory and rational parts of nature. Like a blind person, [the
> person who has entered the dark night] must lean on dark
> faith, accept it as guide and light and rest on nothing of what
> he understands, tastes, feels or imagines.
>
> *— John of the Cross*[6]

This grace-charged night is not a matter of a few short
weeks or months, but of years — often *many* years, depending upon the degree of deprivation and injury the soul has
incurred. Like Magdalen at the tomb, we lament: "They have
taken away my Lord and I do not know where they have put
him" (Jn 20:13).

> Having emerged from the state of beginners, the soul usually
> spends *many years* exercising itself in the state of proficients.
> In this new state . . . the soul goes about the things of God
> with much more freedom and satisfaction of spirit and with
> much more abundant interior delight than before entering
> the night of sense. Without the work of meditation, the soul
> readily finds a very serene, loving contemplation [emphasis
> added].
>
> *— John of the Cross*[7]

The "old man" of St. Paul is being battered, pummeled,
and knocked to the canvas — but he will not stay down for
the full count. He will pick himself up and continue the fight,
only in a different arena, the arena of the *spirit*. There is a
final knock-down drag-out round still to be contested — the
night of the spirit, the purification of the deepest recesses of
the soul, which is not within the purview of this book.

We must first do our part to prepare for the gift of the first
purifying night of sense. By a discipline of prayer, distancing
ourselves from the allurements of the world, by the practice
of the Christian virtues, living a life of simplicity and mod-
eration, practicing recollection, and absorbing Scripture and

solid spiritual reading, we can prepare ourselves for this gift
that comes clothed in the dark and dreary attire of the night
of sense. Without a dedication of this kind *the gift will be
denied us* and given to others more generous, more deeply
desirous of the Lord.

> Although this work [of contemplation] is performed by the
> Lord and we can do nothing to force His Majesty to grant us
> this favor, we can do a great deal to prepare ourselves.
> *— Teresa of Avila*[8]

At the end of the tunnel of the dark night, however, there is
divine light:

> Souls which submissively accept their first trials, enjoy peace
> in a short time, and then the knowledge how to find God in
> darkness. *As a result of this knowledge they make rapid
> progress.* Those who cling to meditation are still waiting after
> thirty or more years of religious life for someone to lift them
> up and show them what they are still searching. They lead a
> colorless and dull life [emphasis added].
> *— Letter of a Carmelite Prioress*[9]

Formerly God communicated himself to us indirectly —
through the senses and our rational faculties. Now God does
so *directly* through our intuitive spiritual faculties:

> God begins to communicate Himself no longer by the senses
> as formerly by means of reasoning, but in a manner purely
> spiritual in an act of simple contemplation.
> *— John of the Cross*[10]

Without death, there is no resurrection. If we would save
our superficial exterior life, we will lose our true inner life
that makes us truly persons and children of God. Unless we
die to self, we cannot live for God. If we do not live for God,
we are already half-dead, though we may believe otherwise.

The Spirit must brood over us and overshadow us if a new creation is to issue out of our darkness — if flowers are to appear in our land, if the season of glad songs is to come, and if the sound of the turtledove is to be heard (Song of Songs 2:12).

> A true love of God is perfectly possible: were it not, all the monasteries and all the Churches on earth would be emptied in a moment and Christianity, for all its framework of ritual, of precepts, of hierarchy, would inevitably crumble away into nothingness. Explain it how one will, the most ardent and most massive blaze of collective love that has ever appeared in the world burns here and now in the heart of the Church.
>   — *Teilhard de Chardin*[11]

22

Presence Is Prayer

Prayer is not a part-time occupation for Christians. There are no part-time contemplatives. To live in the presence of God should be as natural for a Christian as to breathe the air that surrounds us; it is the spontaneous expression of our love of the Lord when we know that we are a child of God.
— *Abhishiktananda (Henri Le Saux, O.S.B.)*

As the contemplative experience deepens, the pervading presence of God becomes more and more habitual. More and more we become a "living prayer." In this clean and simple Presence, all praise, adoration, petition, and thanksgiving become a unity. Enclosed in this silent wordless prayer are all the needs and aspirations of our heart. This prayer reaches out to all for it is Christ praying in us through "the Spirit which has been given us" (Rom 8:15). Like a gentle summer rain that falls on the just and the unjust alike, this prayer seeps into the ground of all humanity, touching all — and is offered back again to God the Rainmaker, along with everyone every drop has kissed.

Once God has taken possession of our hearts, God possesses our total being. There is a Sufi saying that proclaims: "The heart is the whole truth of man." "Our heart is the place," writes George Maloney, "where I take my life in hand and fashion it for good or evil, into what I wish to become." As previously noted, it is the fourth-century Syrian Church Father Pseudo-Macarius who has given us a beautiful and

holistic "theology of the heart," both unitive and contemplative: "I read Macarius and sang!" wrote John Wesley in his
diary.

> The heart itself is a small vessel, yet dragons are there and
> there are also lions; there are poisonous beasts and all the
> treasures of evil. But there, too, is God, the angels, the life
> and the Kingdom, the light of the Apostles, the heavenly
> cities and the treasures of grace.[1]

> Divine grace writes on the "tables of the heart" the laws of
> the Spirit and the heavenly mysteries. The heart directs and
> governs all the other organs of the body. And when grace
> pastures the heart, it rules over all the members and the
> thoughts. For there, in the heart, the mind abides, as well
> as all the thoughts of the soul and all its hopes. This is how
> grace penetrates throughout all parts of the body.[2]

Such a biblical understanding of the heart has been largely
lost in Western Christianity. The Latin word *mens* originally
meant mind *and heart*. Our Western culture has rendered it
simply as "mind" — and we've been in trouble ever since!
Over recent centuries the Western Church has abandoned its
"contemplative heart" and became a religion of the head.
Theologians like Augustine and Aquinas, grounded in the
intellectual Platonism and speculative philosophy of Aristo-
tle, laid the foundation for the Western Church to become
overly speculative and excessively rational-minded. In our
time, many of its thirsting, spiritually deprived people are
leading the Church back to its contemplative roots.

As long as our prayer is active, it admits of separation
between God and ourselves. Teresa of Avila likens discursive prayer to "drinking water that runs along the ground
mixed with mud." In the simplicity of the silent, wordless
"prayer of presence" the ego-I disappears, dissolving subject-
object dualism, leaving unity and union. This, to repeat,
cannot be the result of any intellectual effort or any medi-

tation technique but of a *gifted presence passively received*, and therefore called *infused contemplation.*

> At a certain level when one leaves the psychic realm in which the spirit is active, all movement is at an end, and even prayer itself ceases. This is the perfecting of prayer, and is called spiritual prayer or contemplation.
>
> — *Vladimir Lossky*[3]

23

The Signs We Are Called

❦

> Because the origin of these aridities may not be the sensory
> night and purgation, but sin and imperfection, or weakness
> and lukewarmness, or some bad humor or bodily indisposi-
> tion, I will give some signs for discerning whether the dryness
> is the result of this purgation [the dark night] or one of these
> other defects.
>
> — *John of the Cross*

Those who have read books on the contemplative life have
perhaps encountered the signs that St. John of the Cross gives
for validating the proximate or personal call to contemplation that is accessed in the dark night of the senses. For those
unfamiliar with these signs, we review them briefly here.[1]

In attempting to verify the authenticity of these signs,
John of the Cross warns that care must be taken to ascer-
tain whether or not they are brought on by natural human
causes and conditions (such as melancholy or depression),
which, like a zircon, can "imitate" the qualities of a dia-
mond. Hence, the need for validation by a knowledgeable
guide, one who is a distance from the forest and can "see
the trees" in the daylight of objectivity. Any attempt to di-
agnose ourselves, who are in the midst of the forest, can
easily lead to self-deception and possibly spiritual disaster. In
St. Bernard's words: "He who attempts to lead himself is led
by a fool." The signs given by the Mystical Doctor are not a
matter of having a "few bad days," or months, but are an on-

going, ever-deepening purification (a deprivation of the sense appetites) lasting for several years, and for some for many years. *All three signs must be concurrently present* in order to validate that one is being gifted with the purifying night of sense.

Those called to a strict, cloistered contemplative life will normally experience much greater darkness and aridity than those of us who live in the world. Teresa of Avila confessed that had she known beforehand of the severity of the trials of the passive nights, she would have fled the convent! The great saints and those called to a lofty degree of sanctity will endure trials of a degree not visited upon the rest of us.

However, for those traveling the mystical path in the world, other kinds of trials, temptations, and difficulties are strewn in our paths, all of which can be part of the "nights" and which need to be dealt with and integrated into our journey. These can include suffering and dislocation caused by the injury or death of a loved one, difficulties in marriage, loss of income and financial hardship, and events that bring on psychological pain, to mention only a few of life's possible afflictions. Sometimes, depending upon the kind and severity of the affliction and the spiritual/psychological health of the person, professional counseling may be called for.

Whatever the situation that may arise, however painful, each represents the *possibility for a life-transforming experience,* a new life-enhancing thrust forward rather than a setback, a breakthrough rather than a breakdown. The gifts of faith and fortitude, for which we must pray, come heavily into supportive play in such situations.

The first sign given by John of the Cross is the *loss of satisfaction and consolation* regarding God and "things spiritual." There is a desolation of spirit, making us believe that our spiritual life has "gone to pot," that God has abandoned us. God is so far removed from us (in feeling) that we cannot even remember what it was like to be "close" to God and God to us. What was once sweetness and light has become bitter, dark, and painful. When we turn for solace to

creatures we are met with the same emptiness and dissatis-
faction. We are in an ungodly mess, or so *our feelings* lead
us to believe, for until now, all of our knowledge and love
of God has been by our sense appetites and rational faculties
and was "of the flesh." "It is the spirit that gives life, the flesh
has nothing to offer" (Jn 6:63).

> Souls do not get satisfaction or consolation from the things of
> God, nor do they get any out of creatures either. Since God
> puts a soul in this dark night in order to dry up and purge its
> sensory appetite, He does not allow it to find sweetness or
> delight in anything.
>
> *— John of the Cross*

If it is determined that one is not suffering from melancholy or some passing mood or bodily indisposition, there
must be evidence that the pain being experienced is the anxiety of one who seeks God but can no longer find God (though
God is "nearer" now than ever before). Someone in a melancholy mood or depression would simply want to forego the
quest and retire into self-pity or remorse. After this condition
had passed, that person would continue to seek satisfaction
in creaturely pursuits.

A second sign is that of a sort of "spiritual homesickness."
Our memory reaches back to remind us of happier times,
when our hearts were filled with love for God. We *knew* it because we could *feel* it. Now, whenever we turn to God, God
is no longer "there." We hope with a kind of desperation that
God will return and be the consoling God of yesterday. But
God does not return. He is silent. God is dead.

> The memory ordinarily turns to God solicitously and with
> painful care, and the soul thinks it is not serving God but
> turning back because it is aware of this distaste for the things
> of God.
>
> *— John of the Cross*

If this mute, indistinct painfulness is caused by a solicitude for God who is now "absent" to us, an affliction caused by "love lost," this is a positive sign that God is spreading a cloak over our rational faculties in order to directly infuse loving knowledge. The presence of this solicitousness, the experience of this painful distaste being experienced can be judged as not due to tepidity or "spiritual flabbiness."

> The reason for this dryness is that God transfers His goods and strength from sense to spirit. Since the sensory part of the soul is incapable of the goods of the spirit, it remains deprived, dry and empty.
>
> — *John of the Cross*

The Saint of Carmel observes that this dry and arid food produces an inclination to remain quiet and a desire for solitude away from the meaningless hub-bub of life and the superficial enjoyments and activities of other people. There appears to be a necessary "incubation period" at the outset of this night whereby one aspires to be very much alone. We must take care that this "period of gestation" should not degenerate into spiritual narcissism and a kind of self-satisfying introspection and withdrawal from life that can disguise itself as contemplation.

> Would-be contemplatives must be on their guard against a kind of heavy, inert stupor in which the mind becomes swallowed up in itself. To remain immersed in one's own darkness is not contemplation.
>
> — *Thomas Merton*[2]

The third sign, and the most telling, is our inability to pray and meditate as before. Any attempt at words or thinking about God quickly decomposes before us, turning to dry ash where not even a small spark of light or love can be perceived. We hang "twisting in the wind," pummeled by a dry desert wind, with no one who can comfort us.[3]

[There is a] powerlessness, in spite of one's efforts, to
meditate and make use of the imagination, the interior sense,
as was one's previous custom. God . . . begins to communicate
Himself through pure spirit by an act of simple contemplation
in which there is no discursive succession of thought.

— John of the Cross

It is not a question of our prayer simply becoming dry;
everyone experiences dryness in prayer from time to time.
The condition of which St. John writes is an *outright inability*
to pray or meditate discursively and is ongoing. One simply
cannot meditate as before — at least not without forcing such
discursive prayer to the point of strain and discomfort, which
is the worst possible thing we could do. On the positive side,
there is a *keen though mute desire for God* which is caused
by the *first inpouring of infused contemplation.* O happy
night!

As this state continues and the darkness deepens, our spirit
becomes stronger and increasingly solicitous about not failing God. Our spirit is being "renewed like the eagle's" (Ps
103:5), growing ever stronger in the Lord. Our love, once
gross and sensual, is being transformed and made spiritual.
We are being gifted to love and worship "in spirit and in
truth."

This gift enables us to go beyond the letter of the Gospel
to attain to its spirit and the depths of the mysteries they
express. The formula is no longer a term but a point of
departure. Under the special inspiration of the Holy Spirit the
soul now makes an act of penetrating faith, which is called
an infused act, for it cannot be produced without infused
contemplation.

— Reginald Garrigou-LaGrange[4]

24

Spiritual Direction

❦

> When sensible fervor ceases and souls experience a deadly
> aridity, when they see themselves surrounded by nothing but
> spiritual dangers, difficulties, defects, temptations and evil in-
> clinations, . . . then it is that they learn to distrust themselves,
> to seek someone who can guide them and implore divine aid
> with true humility. No longer do they appropriate to them-
> selves the lights and favors they had received from God. Now
> all their hope lies in perseverance in prayer — cost what
> it may.
>
> — *Juan Gonzales Arintero, O.P.*

When we first cross the obscure and indistinct frontier of
contemplation, we discover a land without roads, devoid of
signposts or familiar landmarks. It is usual in most cases for
contemplation to "sneak up" on us before we become aware
we are traveling in a new country. One day we are awakened to the realization that something is "different" about
us, something "has happened" in our spiritual life, something
"present" that was not there before. Gradually, as this simple presence makes itself known, we begin to realize we have
crossed over into an unknown land, one totally unfamiliar to
us. We are awakened to the reality that God is "invading" us,
that this new "something" is what is called "contemplation."

> A person generally does not perceive this love at the
> beginning, but rather experiences the dryness and void we

are speaking of. Then, instead of this love which is enkindled afterward, in the midst of the dryness and emptiness of the faculties, the person will harbor a habitual care and solicitude for God, accompanied by grief or fear of not serving Him. It is a sacrifice most pleasing to God.

— *John of the Cross*[1]

The horizon itself is blurred so that we cannot see or imagine what lies ahead. This "land of unlikeness" resembles nothing in our past experience and is devoid of anything we can cling to. When we reach for some sort of compass (such as a book on spirituality) it spins mercilessly before us. We are lost and confused. Our confusion might well lead to panic and retreat unless help soon arrives:

If there is no one to understand them, they either turn back and abandon the road, or lose courage, or at least they hinder their own progress because of excessive diligence in continuing to tread the path of discursive meditation. They fatigue and overwork themselves.

— *John of the Cross*[2]

Had we planned a sojourn into the wilds of Africa, we would most certainly have arranged for an experienced guide to lead us, someone who knew the well-traveled paths and the treacherous pitfalls. There is a saying in the East: "When the disciple is ready, the guru will appear." This is a reliable axiom, but not infallible! If we humbly ask God for help, we will get it — although help may not be immediately forthcoming. If help does not arrive, we must remember that the greatest of "spiritual directors" resides deep in our own heart. To hear the whispered counsel of the Holy Spirit, we must be docile and recollected.

Those who are fortunate enough to have a good director who is zealous and intelligent and who will teach them how to remain in silence before our Lord with only a loving glance

and an earnest desire of pleasing Him (for they are unable
to meditate or ask for anything or give expression to their
affections), will, if they are docile, gradually overcome the
obstacles by means of his counsels and encouragements and
will happily pass through this terrible period of trials. Without
such a director they are exposed to great danger.

— Juan Gonzales Arintero, O.P.[3]

In our day, we can substitute a less formal name for
"spiritual director": guide, soul-mate, soul-friend, or spiritual companion. Whoever that person is, he or she must
possess a sound grasp of the mystical life and know it experientially. The guide we choose need not be a priest or a
religious. (Some of the best mystical theologians in the Eastern Church are lay people). Guidance is especially important
at the beginning of the spiritual journey, without which our
first tentative steps can easily cause us to stumble and be led
off into any number of fruitless and divergent directions:

The difficulties that travelers encounter along the spiritual
way are so great, and each of us knows that the ignorance
within us is so vast and insidious, that we all have need of
having some kind of a guide. You need spiritual direction just
to begin the spiritual journey. Without it there is usually no
beginning at all. You will begin to travel unsteadily, unsurely,
and often weighed down by many false principles.

— George A. Maloney[4]

Poor spiritual direction can wreak untold harm. We know,
for instance, that Teresa of Avila suffered for many years at
the hands of incompetent directors, whereas St. Jane Chantal progressed rapidly under the knowledgeable guidance of
her director, St. Francis de Sales. The task of direction requires discretion, prudence, a humility that does not impose
one's own way on another or allow for a desire to control
others, and a profound love of the Lord illumined by one's
own experiential mystical knowledge.

There is perhaps no more difficult and delicate task for a director than the guidance of Christians called to a life of interior prayer. This is rendered all the more arduous by the fact that there is so much pious nonsense written, printed and said about "mystics." Direction is very important in the life of prayer. At the present time the situation is such that the director who is not very simple and very wholesome can do great harm to someone who might be quite close to God in prayer.

— Thomas Merton[5]

St. John of the Cross has no kind words for incompetent directors unschooled in the mystical life, whom he likens to beginners:

It is very important that a person take care into whose hands he entrusts himself. Although the foundation for guiding a soul to spirit is knowledge and discretion, the director will not succeed in leading the soul onward to it . . . if he has no experience of what true and pure spirit is. As a result, many directors cause great harm. . . . Knowing no more than that which pertains to beginners, they do not wish souls to pass beyond these beginnings and these discursive and imaginative ways.[6]

25

Prayer Paths to Contemplation

❧

One of the reasons why contemplative pray-ers have always
been in the minority is because contemplation involves a surrender of one's whole self, not just a period of time each day
devoted to some kind of prayer or meditation. It is a commitment of immense proportions and hence requires trust of an
eminent character, faith that God will bring you to where you
want to go if you submit to this inner conviction or urging that
you have to go. It doesn't matter how many difficulties there
are, you have to go.

— *Thomas Keating, O.C.S.O*

Ancient Christian tradition offers several contemplative
prayer practices that lead to the birthing of a contemplative
spirituality, providing we are faithful to them in a discipline
of daily practice, and providing we make a sincere and conscious effort to bring the fruit of our prayer into the daily
events and activities of life. True contemplative spirituality,
as Thomas Keating states, cannot be isolated to those periods we set aside for prayer, but must water and saturate all
of life.

All true Christian prayer is rooted in Scripture, in *lectio
divina*, where we first encounter God's Self-revelation, written down by human instruments under the influence of the
Holy Spirit. For the Desert and Church Fathers, *lectio divina*
meant more than "divine reading," but, rather, divine *listening* whereby they would create periods of silence during their

reading, opening themselves to the Spirit "imbedded" in the words being read.

All contemplative prayer practices should lead to this open, "active receptivity" where, in faith, we wait upon the Lord in the silent depths of our hearts. In this silence we encounter the transcendent God in the "luminous darkness" of his immanence. Becoming silent and still, we know God without knowing, see God without seeing. There is darkness yet there is light. There is emptiness yet there is fullness. In the poverty of this apparent nothingness, we somehow intuit that we are rich beyond measure. All is wonderment and mystery in this sacred place of receptive silence — even though there often is an utter absence and deprivation of *feelings.*

Contemplative prayer practices are of two general types: those that are focused and concentrated and those that are open and receptive. In the first category fall those prayer practices that make use of the repetition of a word or phrase that in the East is called a mantra. The Jesus Prayer, sometimes called the great Christian mantra, is one of these. The mantra method offered by the Benedictine John Main is another focused or concentrated prayer form.

We do not usually think of the Rosary as a mantra inasmuch as most mantras are short, of one or only a few syllables. One of the great Buddhist mantras, however, consists of one hundred syllables. The "Hail Mary" has about half that number. There is a contemplative way to pray the Rosary, beautifully described by Trappist Basil Pennington in his *Praying by Hand.* Far better to pray a single decade of the Rosary contemplatively than to reel off fifteen decades in one perfunctory brief period.

Centering Prayer, a contemporary name for an ancient practice, falls into the open or receptive category of prayer and is rooted in *The Cloud of Unknowing* and in the Conferences on Prayer of the Desert Father John Cassian. In Centering Prayer, the practitioners initiate a preselected one- or two-syllable word only when they realize that they have been "caught up" in a thought/distraction. The gentle re-introduction of this word helps to reinforce our intention to be open and receptive to God's presence and action in us. All of the focused or concentrated "mantra" prayer paths should lead, through practice and time, to this same open, wordless, active receptivity, this unadorned simple presence before God without words, thoughts, or images.

It is not the purpose of this book to attempt a treatment of the different Christian prayer paths to contemplation, but only to point to the various ancient prayer paths from which we can choose, each according to what attracts and appeals to us. This "attraction" is communicated to us by the Holy Spirit. Accordingly, we have listed some founda-tional writings in the bibliography that treat in depth of the four Christian contemplative prayer practices cited. May the Spirit, in quiet reflective silence, reveal the path each of us is invited to follow that leads to contemplation.

I will come back to you. In a short time the world will no longer see Me, *but you will see Me,* because I live and you will live. On that day you will understand that I am in My Father, and you in Me, and I in you.

—*John 14:18–20*

26

The Long Journey Home

When you are starting out, you must bring everything you
possess — your body, mind and soul. You must take the lot,
your strengths and weaknesses, your sinful past, your great
hopes and your basest and most violent urges. You must take
everything, because everything must pass through fire.

— *Yves Raguin, S.J.*

There are no microwave mystics. There is no instant nir-
vana. There are no thousand-dollar psychobabble California
weekends that will "turn us on" and send us home ready for
canonization. Nor is there any "laying on of hands" that will
resurrect the inner self and launch us into the mystical life.
The masters of the spiritual life insist that the charismatic
experience is a gilt-edge invitation from God to go deeper,
to move beyond "speaking in tongues" to *experiencing God
in silence.* The glossolalia are the lowest of the charisms, as
St. Paul makes clear. St. Thomas tells us that the charisms
are ordained chiefly for the benefit of our neighbors and only
prepare them to be converted, without giving them divine
life.[1] This observation is made without the remotest intention to minimize the charismatic movement, a singular gift
of God, but only to emphasize that there is something deeper
and more profound to which charismatics, and all Christians,
are called, namely, contemplation.

As Thomas Keating points out, whenever fundamentalist
influence has been strong (which is fairly common), there is

a tendency to place special importance on the charismatic gifts (of 2 Cor 2), gifts that can be freely given to anyone *without any corresponding development and growth in that person's spiritual life.* In other words, such gifts are not to be taken as indications of holiness or as marks of spiritual progress. Emphasis upon or attachment to these gifts (which the subtle ego is poised to embrace with sheer delight!) tends toward spiritual pride, which in turn leads to the stagnation and distortion of the spiritual life.

Regarding the relationship between the charismatic movement and the Church's teaching on contemplative prayer, Keating writes:

> While baptism in the Spirit does not establish an advanced stage of spiritual development, it is a manifest call to contemplative prayer. The contemplative tradition of the Church teaches that contemplative prayer is the normal development of the practice of the Christian life. The initial fervor flowing from baptism in the Spirit . . . tends to settle down and turn into dryness in prayer and devotional practices, . . . signs which are the usual introduction of the dark night of sense.
>
> At this crucial period in one's spiritual development, it is important to realize the sharp distinction between charismatic gifts such as tongues, prophecy, healing, etc., and the seven gifts of the Spirit. The charismatic renewal needs spiritual guides who are thoroughly qualified through knowledge and personal experience of contemplative prayer to distinguish what is essential from what is accidental in the spiritual path.[2]

An all-too-prevalent pitfall in the charismatic movement is the tendency, in the face of having received one or more of the charismatic gifts, to believe that this is the highpoint of the spiritual life and that there is no need (for there is no desire) to move beyond. Buttressed by a secret attachment to the gifts, this is akin — though in a much smaller sense — to the reaction of Peter, James, and John on Mt. Tabor, to wit, their desire to permanently stay there and "enjoy the glow." The true "Taboric light" (a profound, sacred experience in the Christian East) is not the glow of the charismatic experience, but is correlative to infused contemplation.

Just as the deepest human love can be expressed only in silence, when we enter into profound intimacy with Christ in God we become *lovingly mute* in an experience that is incommunicable. "He who speaks," the Buddha reminds us, "does not know. He who knows, does not speak" — because he or she *cannot*. We are made tongue-tied and dumb of words, thoughts, and ideas.

Although God, in absolute freedom, can make us saints in seconds, this is not the way God normally chooses. This is God's mercy, for we must stumble and fumble and make mistakes and sometimes even "crash and burn" so that we become convinced beyond any shadow of doubt, beyond any prideful deception, that we are utterly dependent upon Merciful Love.

> At times the Divine Doctor permits these souls . . . to stumble and falter. He does this that they may better realize their own weakness and misery. Sometimes he even lets them suffer a little fall.
> — *Juan Gonzales Arintero, O.P.*[3]

We must simmer on life's stove for a long time and "cook" slowly so that we will be "well done" as we come to the end of our earthly spiritual journey. George Maloney calls it the "slow burn." When once we prepare and dispose ourselves for the gift of contemplation, we can be brought quickly into the night of sense where contemplation is introduced to our experience:

> Not much time ordinarily passes after the initial stages of their spiritual life before beginners enter this night of sense. And the majority of them do enter it because it is common to see them suffer these aridities.
> — *John of the Cross*[4]

Contemplation is not a static state but a dynamic, ever-unfolding gift admitting of infinite growth. The gift of contemplation requires time and great care and vigilance if it is to deepen and gradually transform us.

"If you are waiting for someone to feed you the mystical life with a spoon" comments Merton, "you will wait a long time." There is no way around the mountain, only up its slope. There may be delays and detours and a bridge or two may collapse beneath our feet. God may test our sincerity in different ways. If, at some point along our ascent, we get the poisonous notion that we "have arrived" and decide to relax and "enjoy the view," there is a Buddhist saying worth reflecting upon: "If you think you've reached the top of the mountain, climb higher!"

Those who are content to bathe in the glow of their nascent contemplation are doomed to see the little they have taken away. "Those who do not progress" warns St. Bernard, "fall back." If we have been given the grace to act like adults yet continue to behave like children, the field that contains the pearl of great price, on which we have put a down payment, will be repossessed by the Landlord.

> The proficient who is satisfied to act like a beginner ceases to make progress and becomes a retarded soul. Many retarded souls end by becoming lukewarm, cowardly, and careless.
> In the end they may become hardened and, as a result, it is often more difficult to bring them back to a fervent life than to bring about the conversion of a great sinner.
> — *Reginald Garrigou-LaGrange*[5]

Part Four

Sentinel at the Gate: Guarding the Heart

27

Killing Care

❦

I am telling you not to worry about your life and what you
are to eat, nor about your body and how you are to clothe
it. Look at the birds of the sky. They do not sow or reap or
gather into barns, yet your heavenly Father feeds them. Are
you not worth much more than they? So do not worry about
tomorrow; tomorrow will take care of itself.
                                              — *Matthew 6:25–27, 34*

A priest friend once told me of someone who came up to him
of a Sunday following the Gospel reading above, complain-
ing: "But, Father, I'm not a bird!" There are different ways to
entirely miss the point of a Gospel passage! Constant preoc-
cupation with things transient and mundane blinds our inner
spiritual eye so that seeing we do not see. Like Martha, we
consign ourselves to the "kitchen" while our Divine Guest
awaits us in the receiving room of our heart. Our inner eye
being blinded, our external eye remains wide open, taking
in everything in sight. We thus pour ourselves out through
our senses and become externally minded. The fact that some
people believe there *is* a God is not faith. To believe *in* God
is something else entirely. Many proclaim faith in God; few
trust God. The depth of our faith can be measured by the
degree of our trust, which, in turn, can be gauged by how
much or little we fret over mundane things and common-
place cares. We seem determined to plan out every moment
of our lives in order to assure ourselves we are in control. The

Gospel calls us to deliberately forget about ourselves and our pimply little cares and concerns. This is not possible without *an infused intensification of the gifts of the Spirit,* the seven higher gifts proper to the contemplative/mystical life.

Earlier centuries were less frantic, less compulsive than our own. The fourteenth century of the great German mystic Johannes Tauler was one of those less frenzied times (though the black plague did little to improve the quality of life!). Even in his time, Tauler sadly observed the problem of needless activity, even that which was perceived to be the "work of the Lord." In his homily on the parable of those invited to the banquet but who found all sorts of excuses to stay away, Tauler comments:

> Who could count the number of people who act in the same way? Everyone — I speak not only of lay people but of Bishops and religious — is busy with their affairs. What negotiations and occupations continually distract and absorb the world! The very thought of it is enough to set one reeling! It would be better to die of hunger on the way than to allow ourselves to be encumbered by so many needless occupations.[1]

Many are invited to the banquet to sip the exquisite wine of contemplation but choose not to attend. Superfluous activity and the pursuit of endless diversion keep us bound to the wheels of a perpetual motion machine from which we cannot seem to disengage ourselves. *"O souls created for such grandeur and called thereto,"* cries John of the Cross in *The Spiritual Canticle, "with what do you occupy yourselves?"* Modern men and women, surrounded by infinite possibilities for diversion, cannot seem to stop, or even slow, the treadmill carrying them to nowhere. Even in the seventeenth century, the French scientist and philosopher Blaise Pascal watched his contemporaries in their flight from reality:

> Nothing is so insufferable to man as to be completely at rest, without passions, without business, without diversion. We

then feel our nothingness, our forlornness. our insufficiency, our dependence, our weakness, our emptiness.[2]

If once we would slow down sufficiently to reflect on our condition and recognize the ruins of our inner being, perhaps we would receive the grace to change our system of values. This would be a moment of grace, a time of Mercy descending, our "kairos" — our time of salvation. What if these moments pass us by? What if such a moment never comes again?

So I say to you: ask and it will be given you, seek and you will find, knock and the door will be opened to you. For the one who asks always receives, the one who seeks always finds, the one who knocks will always have the door opened to them.
— *Luke 11:9–11*

28

Idle Curiosity

❧

> Curiosity is a defect of the mind which inclines us toward the consideration of useless subjects, making us neglect the things of God.
>
> — *Reginald Garrigou-LaGrange*

The stepchild of killing care is idle curiosity, which smothers the spiritual life with equal efficiency. The "busy bees" will often be the "busybodies" looking constantly about for fear they will miss something. Little escapes their wandering eyes or their pointed antenna ears. They devour scraps of life around them the way a goat ingests almost anything in its path.

The idly curious read the daily newspaper front to back (the big Sunday paper is a feast day!), take note of every sign and billboard along the road, flip on the radio or TV first thing in the morning to catch the latest news and newsy items. They are now armed for the day. Countless talk shows inundate the airwaves, the vast majority of which are exploitive, giving us the "opportunity" to witness the private pain and sordid experiences of others.

At this writing there are cable systems that can bring in some five hundred TV channels. It is reported that some people who own such mega-systems are experiencing real anxiety trying to decide what to watch! Television, with a menu offering huge servings of insipid sitcoms, steamy sex, and gut-wrenching violence, has "progressed" from once being a "vast wasteland" to being a contaminating cesspool.

Programs that educate and uplift, even inspire, although relatively few in number, are available to the discriminating viewer. In the TV industry there is a dictum: LOP — shorthand for Least Objectionable Programming. Rather than switch off the set, people resignedly watch what is least boring until something more to their liking becomes available. "Bore me" says the LOP viewer, "but don't abandon me!"

The "couch potato" is now one of our more frequently encountered species. Family viewing averages approximately *ten hours a day.*[1] The average child watches some five thousand hours of television before he or she is five years old. Some adults watch three hundred hours of television a month. There is a widespread collective unconditional surrender to the magic box. When regular TV fare fails to win the attention of our children and teens, an unlimited number of TV computer games (some of which, called "virtual reality" programs, are frighteningly sophisticated, violent, and sexually explicit) absorb many additional hours of the days and weeks. Researchers tell us that children are being "stressed out" playing "survivor games" in their attempt to conquer some evil character or force.

In the mythical biblical story of the Tower of Babel, the crisis was the inability to decipher the torrent of words. Our predicament today is precisely the opposite: we *can* decipher the flood of words and process them into understanding. Being able to understand, our minds become great landfills for the scraps of junk food being dished out day after day. Having now become accustomed to ingesting and processing all kinds of garbage, our minds no longer have capacity for what will elevate and enlighten them. We thus become trapped in our own landfill, condemned to live off its chaff and husks.

One day, by a graced intuition, perhaps we will sense our alienation from our true selves. Scanning the inscape of our heart in a quiet reflective moment, perhaps we will have the sense to return to our Father's house and reclaim our birth-right — and ourselves.

> While he was still a long way off, his father saw him and was
> moved with pity. He ran to him, clasped him in his arms, and
> kissed him tenderly.
>
> *— Luke 15:20–21*

29

Carnal-Minded

❧❀❧

The unspiritual are interested only in what is unspiritual, but
the spiritual are interested in things spiritual. It is death to limit
oneself to what is unspiritual; life and peace can only come
with concern for the spiritual.

— *Romans 8:5–7*

The carnal-minded person is not simply one who lusts, or one
driven by greed, or one who thirsts for power and delights in
it — enjoying control of others and intoxicated on the strong
wine of their own self-importance. Carnal minded people are
those who, while not leading a terribly sinful life, are concerned, hour after hour, day after day, with the mundane,
the superficial, the trivial, the transient. Like flies trapped
in a spider's web, they do not have the spiritual energy to
free themselves from the trap. Though only "threads" en-
snare them, they are inescapably bound to this sticky web
they themselves have spun. To live thus alienated from their
true selves is to live in a special kind of insulated hell.
Constantly digging for the gold of happiness and personal
fulfillment, they stumble away carrying fool's gold, leaving
the real motherlode vein untapped.

There are so many Christians who do not appreciate the
magnificent dignity of their vocation to sanctity, to the
knowledge, love and service of God. There are so many
Christians who do not realize what possibilities God has

149

placed in the life of Christian perfection — what possibilities
for joy in the knowledge and love of Him. There are so many
Christians who have practically no idea of the immense love
God has for them, and of the power of that love to do them
good, to bring them happiness.

— Thomas Merton[1]

"The glory of God" St. Irenaeus wrote in the second century, "is the human being fully alive!" Eighteen centuries
later, Flannery O'Connor would write: "Saints are super-
alive people." The spiritual journey is the quest for aliveness
and a release from the shackles of mediocrity that deadens
the spirit and makes us less than truly human.

Man and woman become "super-alive" (it has nothing to
do with a bubbly, effervescent personality!) when the incom-
ing tide of contemplation raises us up off the muddy shoals
in which we had been mired. No longer carnal-minded, our
minds have been "renewed by a spiritual revolution, so that
we can put on the new self that has been created in God's
way, in the goodness and holiness of the truth." (Eph 4:23–
24). Had St. Paul lived in our time, he might have written in
the idiom of modern psychology: "Your minds must undergo
a *transformation of consciousness,*" for this is what contemplation effects — a gradual inner transformation that frees
our imprisoned "inmost I," which has Christ, the Soul of our
soul, as its source and vivifying spirit.

If the inner self is awakened it communicates a new life to
the intelligence where it lives, so that it becomes a living
awareness of itself. And this awareness is not something
that we have, but something that we are. It is a new and
indefinable quality of our living being.

— Thomas Merton[2]

30

A Sea of Lies

❦

We must be saved from immersion in the sea of lies and passions which is called "the world." The creative and mysterious inner self must be delivered from the hedonistic and destructive ego that seeks only to cover itself with disguises.

— *Thomas Merton*

The great intuition of Buddhism and one of its driving forces is the discovery and realization that all the "facts" and conditions of the world are unreal, in the sense that they are impermanent and transitory. Everything is in constant flux of becoming and passing away. Things exist only relatively and conditionally. It is ignorance (*maya*) to see the world of appearances as substantially real. It is enlightenment to see them as only provisionally real. To persist in unreality and live our lives accordingly is enslavement, and even a kind of unrecognized insanity. To see the phenomenal world as transient, impermanent, and provisional is liberation and the beginning of wisdom.

Enlightenment, like contemplation, is not gained through rational thought processes, but by an inner awakening that occurs unexpectedly and that then pervades our life and conditions our attitudes toward life. (We should not make the mistake of deciding that enlightenment and contemplation are the same thing or the same experience, although there are certain general points of commonality, such as the realization of the emptiness and insubstantiality of the phenomenal world around us).

Christianity teaches this same truth, although not with the same single-minded force of Buddhism. Christians would gain much, and our lives would be more purposefully oriented, if we meditated more on this truth, until it so seeped into our consciousness that we would always be aware that the "sea" in which we are immersed is a sea of lies. The documents of Vatican II recognized with approval this underlying truth of Buddhism:

> Buddhism ... realizes the radical insufficiency of this changeable world. It teaches a way by which men and women, in a devout and confident spirit, may be able to either acquire the state of perfect liberation or attain, by their own efforts or through higher help, supreme illumination.[1]

The source of all illusion is, itself, an illusion — the false exterior ego-I, which has no ontological roots and, at death, is doomed to destruction. In the love therapy of purgatory, this false ego-self is transformed into our true, authentic self, becoming transformed and divinized in Christ. For most, however, this false self and the "nothingness" it projects, is where reality "is at," a cruel deception that lures us mercilessly down the twisting dead-end road of ambition and false hopes and dreams. The challenge — and therefore the opportunity — for Buddhist and Christian alike, is to work free of this snare and live in the truly real world.

The ego-I, the "father of lies," feeds on the very lies of its own fabrication, spinning a web of falsity and deception. It believes its own lies, seducing us with *the* great lie from which all other lies are birthed — that you and I and everyone else are isolated, separate, individually sourced "units." What is mine is mine and what is yours I may decide to go after! Thus we live in a divided consciousness, "split off" from everyone and everything else, alienated from our true selves, and therefore from God. In Christian theological terms, this is "original sin."

Like Lazarus in the tomb, our true inner self is encased in darkness and isolation. We must prepare and dispose ourselves so that when our name is called to "come forth," we will be able to hear the Voice that can set us free and remove the fetters that bind us. Contemplatives *experience* the true "freedom of the children of God" (Gal 4:7), being gifted with an experiential certitude that they are truly God's children. Contemplatives live with the habitual enlightened consciousness that there is something greater, something profoundly more "real" than what is right in front of their eyes. This new consciousness is our true inner self being awakened and emerging into consciousness:

> The inner self is not a part of our being; it is our entire substantial reality itself, on its highest and most existential level. It is like life, and it is life. It is our spiritual life when it is most alive. If it is awakened it communicates a new life to the intelligence where it lives so that it becomes a living awareness of itself; and this awareness is not so much something that we have, as something that we are. It is a new and indefinable quality of our living being.
>
> — *Thomas Merton*[2]

When the winds of life swirl about us and storms threaten to inundate us, how quickly and with what utter collapse do our sand castles erode, engulfed by the "sea of lies" we thought was *terra firma*. There is no greater tragedy:

> Our soul seems to continue its weary way, followed endlessly by the multitude of its innumerable trifles, its pretense, its curiosity and vanity. Our soul seems to remain in the marketplace where, from all quarters, the hawkers congregate to sell the petty goods of this world and where, in stultifying restlessness, men and women wander about offering their trifles.

One day after the other we go on like this to the hour of our death, when all the goods and chattels which we called "our life" will be swept away. What will we be then? What will remain of us whose life was nothing but the business of the day, of idle talk and vain pretense?

— *Karl Rahner*[3]

31

Contemplation and Compassion

☙❧

Christian self-realization can never be a merely individualistic affirmation of one's isolated personality. Charity, which is the life and awakening of the inner self, is in fact awakened by the presence and spiritual influence of other selves that are "in Christ." In a word, the awakening of the inner self is purely the work of love, and there can be no love where there is not "another" to love.

— Thomas Merton

True contemplation by its very nature reaches out to others in compassion, the fruit of love and the highest expression of love, which finds its authenticity in service, in the care of the needs of others, be they physical, psychological, or spiritual. A contemplation that reposes in its own isolation is, by every legitimate Christian yardstick, a counterfeit contemplation unworthy of the name. Contemplation — the gift of the Holy Spirit — *impels us* by that same Spirit to reach out to others. For some, it is validated by a dedication to corporal works of mercy, for others by the call to a wide variety of other gifts of the Spirit who is now the animating and directing life of our being.

To some, the gift was that they should become apostles; to some prophets; to some, evangelists, to some pastors and teachers, so that the saints together make a unity in the work of service, building up the body of Christ. In this way we are

155

all come to unity in our faith and in our knowledge of the Son
of God, until we become the perfect Man, fully mature with
the fullness of Christ Himself.

— Ephesians 4:11–13

A humorous story from the lives of the Desert Fathers is
illustrative:

> A brother asked one of the elders: "There are two brothers,
> one of whom remains at prayer in his cell, fasting six days at
> a time and doing a great deal of penance. The other, after
> praying, goes and takes care of the sick brethren. Which
> one's work is most pleasing to God?" The elder replied: "If
> the brother who prays all the time and fasts and does great
> penance were to do so hanging by his nose, he could not
> equal the one who takes care of the sick!"
> *— Verba Seniorum (Migne Collection)*

We cannot *love* a "higher power" or a "universal intelligence" or a "cosmic mind." Human beings cannot love an
"it" or an impersonal entity, since there is no personal contact point of deep mutuality between a "love-being" and
an "it-being." We may receive illuminations and enlighten-
ments, but they have little to do with love *unless* we are led
deeper to the "supra-Person" at the ground and source of all.
Christian contemplation and the mystical life are a matter
of love, grounded in a living personal God who *is* love. In
Karl Rahner's words: "God gives himself in his own reality
in self-communication to man as man's own fulfillment." In
St. Paul's words: "In him [the person of Christ], you too find
your own fulfillment" (Col 2:9).

Love, as Merton reminds us, is our identity, love is our
name. True love cannot be something impersonal or have its
genesis in an impersonal source. "In order to love," Merton
writes, "there must be another to love." Created for love and
to *be* love, we cannot become fully human without love being *gifted* to us in ever-increasing abundance, "grace upon

grace." We are loved into full being and in no other way. Sin is the refusal of this love.

We need not take on great tasks or engage in noble causes. What we do in the service of others can be externally insignificant, but, if motivated by love for the One who sacrificed himself for us, "though it be as insignificant as an ant" (Abbé Monchanin), it assumes great power and is worth much in the sight of God. "In the evening of our life," John of the Cross reminds us, "we will be judged not by our works but by our love." With the gift of contemplation comes the responsibility to act in accordance with the magnitude of the gift, for we never receive it exclusively for ourselves but to serve others.

> Christian contemplation cannot consist merely in a dark withdrawal into subjective peace, without reference to the rest of the world. A contemplation which hides in subjectivity and individualism is a by-product of bourgeois spirituality. It is a comfortable negation of the present life, which is not really a negation of anything but only an evasion of responsibility in order to enjoy interior comfort.
>
> — *Thomas Merton*[1]

The celebrated fourteenth-century English mystic Walter Hilton advises us to "throw some sticks of wood" (active service) against the "little coal of fire" (contemplation) burning within us, so that this delicate love will not "grow cold in idleness for want of fuel."[2]

Those who might be described as "active livers," who claim they have little or no time for prayer, deceive themselves — a transparent "cop-out" in the guise of being "realistic and practical." Without a discipline of prayer/ meditation, their ministry will turn hollow and unfruitful, eventually degenerating into a reluctant, mechanical functioning, devoid of unction, empty of lasting results, and bankrupt of compassion — in short, *a ministry that is essentially un-Christian.*

Even those in the active life should strive for contemplation.
Prayer is no less necessary for them. If the conditions of this
life render the highest forms of contemplation inaccessible,
its substance is not refused them. On the contrary, Our Lord
invites all.

— *Reginald Garrigou-LaGrange*[3]

LaGrange makes the point that "religious and priestly
lives, which might be very fruitful, do not go beyond a certain
mediocrity" for lack of a life of prayer and contemplative
grounding. Merton uses the apt analogy of the spring and the
stream, representing the contemplative and the active life of
ministry. Unless the stream of our ministry is fed by the living
waters of contemplation, the stream, cut off from its source,
will soon dissipate and dry up, or, at best, become a trickle
incapable of irrigating the fields of our ministries.

There have been times past when the Gospel story of
Martha and Mary has been interpreted to read "either/or" —
with the contemplative life, the "better part," split off as
supremely more meritorious and desirable. St. Bernard reminds us that Martha and Mary "are sisters" and should
not be separated. Our Lord's rebuke of Martha hinges not on
the fact she was busy "sweating over a hot stove," but that
she did not take time from her chores to contemplate Truth,
which was right in front of her. We, who are tempted to seek
activity as an *escape* from prayer and periods of solitude,
need be mindful that not only is Truth "right in front of us,"
but intimately *within* us, awaiting our undivided attention.

The refusal of those engaged in the active life to set aside
time for prayer, to "contemplate Truth," makes for a medi-
ocre and joyless life — a life that soon becomes bothersome,
wearisome, and personally unrewarding. However, the contemplative who does not eventually reach out to others in
compassionate service faces an even more foreboding fate:

Solitude is necessary for spiritual freedom. But once this
freedom is acquired [through the inner awakening that is

contemplation], it demands to be put to work in the service of a love in which there is no longer subjection or slavery. Mere withdrawal, without the return to freedom in action, would lead to a static and death-like inertia of the spirit in which the inner self would not awaken at all. There would be no light, no voice within us — only the silence and darkness of the tomb.

— *Thomas Merton*[4]

32

Cautions and Counsels

❧❧❧

In his last unpublished "will and testament" "The Inner Experience," Thomas Merton punctuated his manuscript with cautions and counsels regarding the contemplative life and the search for transcendent experience. Merton's insights and observations are jewels of practical and sober reflection that, if thoughtfully read, will contribute to keeping the seeker safely grounded and sanely oriented. After working and reworking the manuscript during the last years of his life, he completed it just prior to his departure for Asia. These "pensées" from "The Inner Experience" represent some of Merton's most mature thought.

Merton applied with practical wisdom what his contemplation and mystical experience taught him. These counsels are published here as a collection for the first time. Like the wisdom of his spiritual father, Bernard of Clairvaux, which stretches down to us over the ages, these are timeless "wisdom counsels" offered by a prophet of our own times and the most human of men, Merton of Gethsemani.

•

The first thing you have to do before you start thinking about such a thing as contemplation is to try to recover your basic natural unity, to reintegrate your compartmentalized being into a coordinated and simple whole, and learn to live as a unified person. This means that you have to bring back together the fragments of your distracted existence so that when you say "I" there is someone really present to support the pronoun you have uttered.

It is surely legitimate for anyone to desire and seek this fulfillment, this experience of reality, this entrance into truth. Let anyone desire it providing only that he is sincere and prudent and open to the truth. The great obstacle to contemplation is rigidity and prejudice. He who thinks he knows what it is beforehand prevents himself from finding out the true nature of contemplation since he is not able to change his mind and accept something new.

The inner self is as secret as God and, like Him, it evades every concept that tries to seize hold of it with full possession. It is a life that cannot be held and studied as object, because it is not a "thing." It is not reached and coaxed forth from hiding by any process under the sun, including meditation. All that we can do with any spiritual discipline is produce within ourselves something of the silence, the humility, the detachment, the purity of heart and the indifference which are required if the inner self is to make some shy, unpredictable manifestation of its presence.

In Christianity, the inner self is simply a stepping stone to an awareness of God. Man is the image of God and his inner self is a kind of mirror in which he is reflected. Thus, through the dark, transparent mystery of our own inner being we can, as it were, see God "through a glass."

Freedom to enter the inner sanctuary of our being is denied to those who are held back by dependence on self-gratification and sense satisfaction, whether it is a matter of pleasure-seeking, love of comfort, or proneness to anger, self-assertion, pride, vanity, greed and all the rest.

He who thinks contemplation is lofty and spectacular cannot receive the intuition of a supreme and transcendent Reality which is, at the same time, immanent in his own ordinary self.

If we enter into ourselves and find our true self, and then pass beyond the inner "I," we sail forth into the immense darkness in which we confront the "I AM" of the Almighty.

There is an infinite metaphysical gulf between the "I" of the Almighty and our own inner "I." Yet, paradoxically, our inmost "I" exists in God and God dwells in it. We must know that the mirror is distinct from the image reflected in it. The Christian mystical experience is not only an awareness of the inner self but also, by a supernatural intensification of faith, it is an experiential grasp of God as present within our inner self.

The problem of contemplation for the average modern man is then a problem of preparation. The average man of our time is disposed to be a "contemplative in reverse," a "mystic" of technocracy or business.

The contemplative life is a matter of great importance to modern man, and it is important to him in all that is most valuable in his ideal. Today more than ever man in chains is seeking emancipation and liberty. His tragedy is that he seeks it by means that bring him into ever greater enslavement.

It seems right to say that one who wants a contemplative life today must do two things: First, he must, as far as possible, reduce the conflict and frustration in his life by cutting down contact with the "world" and his secular subjections. This means reducing his needs for pleasure, comfort, re-creation, prestige, and success, and embracing a life of true spiritual poverty and detachment. Secondly, he must learn to put up with the inevitable conflicts that remain — the noise, the agitation, the crowding, the lack of time and, above all, the constant contact with a purely secular mentality which is all around us everywhere and at all times, even to some extent in monasteries.

It is therefore a matter of great courage and spiritual energy to turn away from diversion and prepare to meet, face to face, that immediate experience of life which is intolerable to the exterior man. This is only possible when we are able to see our inner selves not as a vacuum but as an infinite depth, not as emptiness but as fullness. This change of perspective is impossible as long as we are afraid of our own nothingness, as long as we are afraid of fear, afraid of poverty, afraid of boredom — as long as we run away from ourselves.

Excursions into the recollected darkness of contemplation are tempting to anyone with a schizoid character, because it is easy to mistake schizoid withdrawal for contemplative recollection.

Is it possible that by the sacrifice of seemingly good economic opportunities you could move into the country or some small town where you would have more time to think? This would involve the acceptance of a relative poverty perhaps. If so, all the better for your interior life.

Wherever you may be it is always possible to give yourself the benefit of those parts of the day which are quiet because the world does not value them. One of these is the small hours of the morning. The dawn is, by its very nature, a peaceful, mysterious and contemplative time of day — a time when one naturally pauses and looks with awe at the eastern sky. It is a time of new life, new beginning and therefore important to the spiritual life; for the spiritual life is nothing but a perpetual interior renewal.

To praise the contemplative life is not to reject every other form of life, but to seek a solid foundation for every other human striving. Without the silence and recollection of the interior life, man loses contact with his real sources of energy, clarity and peace.

If your contemplation is a complete blank or a mere spiritual chaos, without any love or desire for God, then be persuaded that you are not a contemplative.

Be content to remain in loneliness and isolation, dryness and anguish waiting upon God in darkness. Your inarticulate longing for Him in the night of suffering will be your most eloquent prayer. But be persuaded, that on the contrary, God is here working to raise your intellect and will to the highest perfection of supernatural activity in union with His Holy Spirit.

Withdraw yourself from all care, trust not in yourself but in Him, do not be anxious or solicitous to perform great works for Him until he leads you Himself to undertake the works He has planned for you and by which He will use you to communicate the fire of His love to other men.

It is clear that if a dialogue is to take place between Christians and the subjectivists of our time, a contemplative is the one to speak for Christianity. A dogmatist, firmly entrenched in scholastic categories, has no way of making himself understood.

The one great danger that confronts every man who takes the spiritual life seriously, is the danger of illuminism. Here the problem is that of taking one's subjective experience so seriously that it becomes more important than the truth, more important than God. Once spiritual experience becomes objectified, it turns into an idol. To live for spiritual experience is slavery, and such slavery makes the contemplative life just as secular (though in a more subtle way) as the service of any other "thing," no matter how base: money, pleasure, success. Indeed the ruin of many contemplatives has been this avidity for spiritual success. What matters is not what one feels, but what really takes place beyond the level of feeling or experience.

Contemplation does not back away from reality, or evade it. It sees through superficial being and goes beyond it. This implies a full acceptance of things as they are, and a sane evaluation of them. The "darkness" of the contemplative night is not a rejection of created things. On the contrary, the contemplative in some way "finds" and discovers things as they really are, and enjoys them in a higher way, when he rises above contacts with them that are merely sensual and superficial.

For the married Christian, his married life is essentially bound up with his contemplation. It is by his marriage that he is situated in the mystery of Christ. It is by his marriage that he bears witness to Christ's love for the world, and in his marriage that he experiences that love. His marriage is a sacramental center from which grace radiates out into every part of his life. The union of man and wife in nuptial love is a sacred and symbolic act, the very nature of which signifies the mystery of the union of God and man in Christ. This mystery is the very heart of contemplation.

33

Woman Who Weeps

❦

Mary stands as the sign of the distinct quality of the Christian Church, holding out to each individual a synthesis of the perfect human being. She is the "place" where transcendence and immanence meet. She opens her whole being in silent contemplation of the awesome, majestic God and she hungers to receive of His fullness. She embraces, womb-like, God's gift of Himself.

— George A. Maloney

In those apparitions that have been declared authentic by the Western and Eastern Church, the Blessed Virgin has often revealed a deep sadness at the state of humankind, alienated from God and her Son. At times she has been seen to weep over the calamitous condition of her children.

Carl Jung, a Protestant, sees the rejection of devotion to Mary by his fellow Protestants as an opportunity lost. Those who reject Mary, Jung states, are sacrificing the opportunity for individuation, for "healing unto wholeness." Sacrificed on the altar of our lopsided ego is the psychic feminine principle of the *anima,* which both balances and completes our humanity. Jung goes on to say that Catholics (and Orthodox Christians) have a unique possibility of uniting the conscious and the unconscious — in a word, to achieve individuation. It is that "part" of us that makes "contact" with God whereby we are united to God. "The human person," George Maloney writes, "becomes a true Christian through his or her *feminine power* of contemplation."

We need not search far in any century to come upon writings of the saints of the Western and Eastern Churches declaring the glories and gifts of the Holy Virgin. In the Eastern Church she is addressed as "Lady Theotokos," or "God-bearer."[1] God-bearer! Was ever there a vocation so great, a dignity so noble, a mission so holy as to be chosen the Vessel of God, the Ark of the Christ-covenant? Her salvific role is part of "the hidden plan which God so kindly made in Christ from the beginning" (Eph 1:19). Mary is the embodiment and the perfection of the Beatitudes. We, her children, are "beatitudes in process."

Sadly, the Western Church has lost the feminine aspect of God and has watched the metaphor for tender care and merciful love, called "Father," degenerate into a depiction of masculine gender. The Eastern Churches, rooted in the Oriental and Greek Fathers, have often ascribed the feminine principle to God the Holy Spirit, "Hagia Sophia," Holy Wisdom. Eastern Orthodoxy has never had to deal with the false problem of whether God is masculine or feminine, understanding that God is both and neither, but is pure Spirit transcending gender and beyond all anthropomorphic interpretations.

Inasmuch as this book treats of the call to the mystical life and the journey to contemplation, one might inquire "is there a shortcut to contemplation?" Saints and theologians attest there is indeed — the "road of Mary" — a road that leads more directly and more swiftly to intimate union with God in Christ. As St. Louis de Montfort, in concord with other saints, assures us:

> The road of Mary is easier, yet nevertheless more meritorious, and consequently a more perfect, short and sure road. One can in truth reach divine union by other roads, but it will be by many more crosses, with many more difficulties, which we shall have to conquer with greater difficulty.[2]

Evidence of this appears in the lives of St. Ephrem the Syrian, John Damascene, Bernard of Clairvaux, Bonaventure, Bernardine of Siena, Francis de Sales, and Francis of Assisi, to whom Christ said in a vision: "Advise your sons to go by the ladder of My Mother."

> What seems to us very complicated, perhaps very subtle in the works of men and their minute analysis is accomplished with extraordinary simplicity and sometimes astonishing rapidity by the Mother of Fair Love.
> — *Thomas Philippe, O.P.*[3]

True devotion to Our Lady has little to do with membership in a Marian group or organization, nor is there any affinity with sentimentality. True devotion has to do with faithful response to the Gospel and the prompt doing of God's will as it is expressed in the concrete events and persons encountered in life, even — and especially — when aridity and darkness weigh heavily upon us.

True filial devotion to Mary is a *gift from Her Son.* After meditating upon the little Scripture has to say about her (the Queen of Contemplatives lived a hidden life), we must address her with humility and faith, asking her to reveal herself to us as loving mother and guide. She will, in turn, lead us into the deeper realms of the interior life, revealing her Son to us as an experience in the depths of our hearts.

The gift of Mary may be taken as a sign of predilection, a sign we are called to the contemplative/mystical life. We dare be so bold as to suggest that she is, as it were, the "eighth gift of the Holy Spirit," containing the seven seeds of wisdom, knowledge, fortitude, piety, understanding, counsel, and reverential fear of the Lord — gifts necessary to our salvation, which are united to charity and grow with charity. In a world that is violently aggressive, power-hungry, manipulative, dominating, destructive and unforgiving, nothing would be more saving and healing than for humankind to awaken to its anima: the open, receptive, nurturing feminine principle that lies smoldering beneath the ashes of a distorted collective psyche. In his typically audacious and striking way of putting things, Meister Eckhart wrote: "For man to become fruitful, he must become a woman! That is the noblest word that can be addressed to the soul." Eckhart obviously is not recommending a sex change (!) but an interior transformation of heart and mind, without which our world and ourselves can never be healed, can never achieve wholeness and individuation. We must recover our true inner selves, stamped with the image and likeness of God.

True devotion to the Lady Theotokos will work in us this restoration of our original unity, "knitting" us back together unto wholeness. We can diminish the tears of the glorified Maiden of Nazareth by genuine devotion to her and living the counsels and commandments of her Son. Faithful and trusting of her, we can experience and live by the words Nuestra Señora de Guadalupe spoke to the young Aztec Indian, Juan Diego, on the rocky slope of Tepeyac Mexico, over 450 years ago:

Listen, and let it penetrate your heart, my dear son. Let nothing discourage you, nothing depress you, let nothing alter your heart or your countenance. Do not fear any illness or vexation or pain. Am I not here, your Mother? Are you not under my shadow and protection? Am I not the fountain of your life? Are you not in the folds of my mantle and in the embrace of my arms? Is there anything else you need?[4]

34

Song of the Butterfly

Long ago in ancient China there was a great sage named Chuang Tzu who once dreamed he was a butterfly. When he awoke, he realized he was not a butterfly, but only Chuang Tzu. However, upon reflection, he was not quite sure. Was it he, he asked himself, who dreamed of being a butterfly, or was he a butterfly who dreamed of being Chuang Tzu? Thus it was that, in dreaming and waking, the song of the butterfly came to be Chuang Tzu's constant companion to his life reflection and to his zestful living.

Did you know that butterflies can sing? Of course, one must be a butterfly to hear their honeyed song. You and I are invited to become butterflies, and not just in our dreams. True, we must start out as caterpillars, plodding slowly along life's journey, some starting out by crawling from word to word, thought to thought, in discursive prayer and meditation.

Caterpillars feed on leaves and other foliage and drink water muddied by the ground, while around them butterflies alight on fragrant flowers and drink their sweet nectar. And as for appearances — not even Solomon in all his glory was arrayed like a butterfly! As they are carried along by the *ruah,* the breath of their Creator, they sing their silent sweet psalmody of contemplation.

Sad to say, through ignorance or indifference, most caterpillars prefer to remain so, crawling along the ground, content with their slow progress, yet feeling secure. Caterpillars can see ahead of them and on both sides, having six eyes on each of their sides, thus eliminating risks as they plod along. Butterflies have no idea where they are or where they are going. They are like the tiny English sparrow that takes off each year into the unknown, migrating over vast spaces and even the ocean itself where no landmark ever appears, buffeted by storms and risking the elements. Yet their Father who provides for them always leads them safely and unerringly home.

No caterpillar can ever hear the song of the butterfly, nor ever taste the nectar from the Garden of the Lord, nor ever know what it is like to be borne aloft by the *ruah,* the Holy Breath. If you don't believe me, then listen to one of the most beautiful and exquisite butterflies who ever flew:

> If you desire I tell you about the way that leads to contempla-
> tion, you must bear with me if I enlarge upon such matters.
> If you don't wish to hear about them, and put them into
> practice, then stay with your mental [discursive] prayer for all
> your whole life, for I assure you — and all persons who aim at
> true contemplation — that you will not thereby reach it.
>
> — *Teresa of Avila*[1]

For a caterpillar to be transformed into a butterfly, it must allow the dark night of the chrysalis to enshroud it. There, it must wait patiently in trusting passivity while the work of transformation is being darkly, secretly accomplished. It must not attempt to analyze what is happening or think or make judgments. It must simply "be" in that darkness, waiting peacefully in Christian hope, for the day — which it has not been given to know beforehand — when it will emerge a winged adult and effortlessly lift itself on painted wings to heights above.

> Not too fast, not too fast
> let it grow, let it last
> Nature knows when and where . . . the butterfly

I remember one morning when I saw a
cocoon in the bark of a tree.
I remember I marveled that imprisoned inside
was a butterfly waiting to be free

I was very impatient so I warmed the cocoon
with the breath of my sighs
And the butterfly trembled and began to emerge
like a miracle right before my eyes.

> — *Sr. Therese Even,*
> *"The Butterfly"*

The poem goes on to say that because the birthing process
of the butterfly was rushed, the butterfly died. This wondrous
work of God takes time — God's time. No wishful thinking,
no study, no meditation or ascetic exercise can transform us
into butterflies. All we can do is prepare ourselves and remain open in Christian hope to the Giver of Gifts, trusting of
Merciful Love.

All we can do with any spiritual discipline is produce within
ourselves something of the humility, the silence, the detachment, the purity of heart and the indifference which are
required if the inner self is to make some shy, unpredictable
manifestation of its presence.

> — *Thomas Merton*[2]

Contemplation is the gift of One who *deeply desires us
to possess it* (although, in fact, it possesses *us*). Yet we
must cooperate and contribute our share. It is the *praxis*
of our prayer, meditation, recollection and *lectio divina* and
the practice of the Christian virtues (the greatest asceticism)
that prepares our inner soil for the planting of the seeds of
contemplation.

My brother, my sister: your parish, your diocese, your
Church is overpopulated with caterpillars! Your Church
needs more butterflies. Come, let us be one of them! Let

us sing the song of the butterfly! It always has been the butterflies who have renewed the Church, who have changed vast regions of the planet. Though ever so delicate and vulnerable, butterflies are the most powerful of God's creatures. One day, on the wings of countless butterflies, the earth — the cosmos itself — will be transported to the Omega point. Then will the Lord of the Butterflies say: "Father, together, we have finished the work You gave us to do. Now all is truly one, all has been perfected in unity. Now, Father, let them share in My glory, your gift to Me, for You have loved us before the foundation of the world" (see Jn 17:4–5, 24).

Let those who are great actives and think to girdle the earth with their outward works, take note that they would bring far more profit to the Church and be far more pleasing to God if they spent even half this time in prayer. Of a surety, they would accomplish more with one piece of work than they now do with a thousand and with far less labor. A very little of this pure prayer is precious in the sight of God and of greater profit to the Church than are all works together.

—*John of the Cross*[3]

Epilogue

The message of hope the contemplative offers you . . . is not that you need to find your way through the jungle of language and problems that today surround God; but that whether you understand or not, God loves you, is present to you, lives in you, dwells in you, calls you, saves you, and offers you an understanding and light which are like nothing you ever found in books or heard in sermons. The contemplative has nothing to tell you except to reassure you and say that if you dare to penetrate your own silence and dare to advance without fear into the solitude of your own heart, and risk the sharing of that solitude with the lonely other who seeks God through you and with you, then you will truly recover the light and the capacity to understand what is beyond words and beyond explanations because it is too close to be explained. It is the intimate union in the depths of your own heart of God's spirit and your own secret inmost self, so that you and He are, in all truth, one Spirit.

> *— Thomas Merton, "Message of the Contemplative to the World." Requested by Paul VI and read to the Synod of Bishops, Rome, 1964*

Appendix

The Promises of Christ

❧

Christian contemplation is grounded in faith — faith not only in God and revelation, but faith also in the explicit promises God has made to us through his Son, Jesus Christ, who is Truth itself. Serious reflection on the Gospel and the Letters clearly reveals the manifest promises of Christ calling us to union with him in this life.

As the theologians and the saints teach, the commandment to "be perfect as your heavenly Father is perfect" (Mt 5:48) is meant for all, the perfection of love. The theological gift of charity is developed and perfected only in the mystical life. There are not "two ways" to sanctity, one ascetic/active and the other mystical/contemplative. Saints like Teresa of Avila and John of the Cross (Doctors of the Church, whose teachings the Church therefore applies to all the faithful) insist that progress in the virtues is proportionate to progress in prayer and contemplation.

The following selected New Testament passages invite us to drink of the "living waters" and enter into the divine nuptials.

•

Let anyone who thirsts come to me! Let anyone who believes in me come to me and drink! As scripture says: "from his heart shall flow streams of living water."

—John 7:38

174

If you only knew what God is offering and who it is that is saying to you: "Give me to drink," you would have been the one to ask, and he would have given you living water. . . . And the water that I shall give will turn into a spring within you, welling up into eternal life.

—John 4:10, 14

Those who receive my commandments and keep them will be the ones who love me; and those who love me will be loved by my Father, and I shall love them and show myself to them . . . and we shall come and make our home with them.

—John 14:21, 23

This is eternal life: to know you, the only true God, and Jesus Christ whom you have sent.

—John 17:3

May they all be one, Father. May they be one in us, as you are in me and I am in you.

—John 17:21

I shall ask the Father and he will give you another Advocate to be with you forever, the Spirit of truth. . . . He is with you, he is in you. In a short time the world will no longer see me; but you will see me, because I live, and you shall live.

—John 14:16–19

The Spirit himself and our spirit bear united witness that we are children of God.

—Romans 8:16

The proof that you are children of God is that God has sent the Spirit of his Son into our hearts, the Spirit that cries "Abba, Father."

—Galatians 4:6

In his body lives the fullness of divinity, and in him you too find your own fulfillment.

—Colossians 2:9

Before the world was made, he chose us, chose us in Christ, to be holy and spotless, and to live through love in his presence.

— Ephesians 1:4

Do you not know that you are God's temple and that God's Spirit lives in you?

— 1 Corinthians 3:16

And we, who with unveiled faces all contemplate the glory of the Lord, are being transformed into his likeness with ever-increasing glory, which comes from the Lord.

— 2 Corinthians 3:18

Out of his infinite glory may he give you the power through his Spirit for your hidden self to grow strong . . . until experiencing the love of Christ which is beyond all human knowledge, you will be filled with the utter fullness of God.

— Ephesians 3:16, 19

Notes

❦

1. Mysticism as Ordinary

1. Thomas Merton, "The Inner Experience," chap. 1. Published as an edited offprint serialized over eight issues of *Cistercian Studies*, 1983–85. Quotations are from the original manuscript.

2. Thomas Merton, *Life and Holiness* (New York: Herder and Herder, 1963), chap. 2, sec. 4.

3. Benedict XV, letter to Reginald Garrigou-LaGrange (September 15, 1921). Reginald Garrigou-LaGrange was a preeminent French Dominican dogmatic/mystical theologian (d. 1964) renowned for his syntheses of the mystical theology of Thomas Aquinas, John of the Cross, and Teresa of Avila. LaGrange taught mystical theology at the Pontifical University in Rome from 1909 to 1960. Like the great Spanish Dominican theologian before him, Juan Gonzales Arintero (1860–1928), LaGrange vigorously insisted on the universal call to infused contemplation and the mystical life as the normal development of the Christian life.

4. Thomas Merton, *What Is Contemplation?* (Springfield, Ill.: Templegate Publishers, 1981), 11.

5. Thomas Merton, private audio tape, unpublished.

6. Karl Rahner, "Mysticism: Nature and History," *Encyclopedia of Theology* (New York: Seabury Press, 1975).

2. Two Bloodied Words

1. At the outset, this presence is not constantly habitual, but "habitual intermittently," becoming more and more habitual as the contemplative life deepens. In the final stages of the mystical life, this presence becomes immutable, even during the most intensive activity and the most demanding of duties. It should be noted that there are contemplatives who do not *know* they are contemplatives, as St. Thomas teaches, simply because they have never heard of "contemplation" but nonetheless live in

the simple habitual presence of God. Merton calls such people "masked contemplatives."

2. Bernard McGinn, *The Foundations of Mysticism,* vol. 1 (New York: Crossroad, 1991), 286. Karl Rahner (1904–84) is considered by many the greatest theologian of the twentieth century. Sometimes called a "pastoral theologian," Rahner was acutely concerned that theology respond to the vital questions and problems of each age and that the theologian should be a pastoral guide and spiritual director, bringing light to ordinary Christians confronting life's complex problems and challenges. He taught, following the Fathers, that knowledge of the Trinity and the mysteries of faith is granted, though obscurely, in mystical experience.

3. Thomas Merton, *New Seeds of Contemplation* (New York: New Directions, 1961), 1–13. The first two chapters of *Seeds* offers a comprehensive exploration of what contemplation is not and of what it consists.

4. Ibid., 6.

5. Reginald Garrigou-LaGrange, *Christian Perfection and Contemplation* (New York: Herder and Herder, 1937), 77.

3. All Who Thirst

1. Teresa of Avila, *The Way of Perfection,* chap. 19, art. 2.

2. Thomas Merton, "Message of the Contemplative to the World." In 1964, Pope Paul IV asked Merton to compose a message of contemplatives to the world to be read at the World Synod of Bishops gathered in Rome toward the close of Vatican II. This message is reprinted in its entirety in *The Monastic Journey,* ed. Patrick Hart, O.C.S.O. (Kansas City, Mo.: Sheed, Andrews and McMeel, 1977), 174.

4. The Greatest Sin

1. George A. Maloney, S.J., "Inscape," monthly teaching on prayer, September 1993.

2. Although there are Protestant mystics, there is no mystical tradition in Protestantism. On the contrary, the vast majority of Protestant theologians consider mysticism a "disease" that has infected the Christian faith. The great German historian of theology Adolf von Harnack (d. 1930) wrote that "mysticism as a rule is rationalism worked out in a fantastic way." The most notable exception to Protestant antipathy toward mysticism was the renowned Dr. Albert Schweitzer, whose "The Mysticism of Paul the Apostle" is a most powerful and persuasive de-

fense of mysticism. See Bernard McGinn's *The Foundations of Mysticism* (New York: Crossroad, 1991), 266–75.

3. Juan Gonzales Arintero, O.P., *The Mystical Evolution and the Development and Vitality of the Church* (New York: Herder & Herder, 1951), 2:413. Arintero (1860–1928) was a Spanish Dominican mystical theologian who did much to retrieve the true Christian teaching on contemplation. He became embroiled in controversy as a result of teaching the call of all Christians to perfection and the normal development of the life of grace into contemplation. His beatification is pending. On his deathbed, Arintero uttered these words: "Within a few hours I shall be brought before the tribunal of God, and I assure you that our teachings concerning contemplation are the true doctrines and that they represent the traditional Christian teachings. But the contrary doctrines are deviations which serve only to mislead souls."

4. Karl Rahner, *The Shape of the Church to Come* (New York: Crossroad, 1974), 85.

5. We follow certain Greek Fathers and Meister Eckhart, who ascribed the feminine gender to the Holy Spirit (Hagia Sophia), Holy Wisdom.

6. Thomas Keating, O.C.S.O., "Vision Statement to Contemplative Outreach," 1993, privately distributed. Keating was abbot of the Trappist Monastery of St. Joseph's Abbey in Spencer, Mass., for some twenty years. In the mid-1970s, he started the Centering Prayer movement. After retiring as abbot, he relocated to St. Benedict's Monastery in Snowmass, Colo., where he founded Contemplative Outreach Ltd. for the purpose of propagating the Centering Prayer teaching worldwide. He is the author of several books on Centering Prayer and contemplative spirituality.

7. Thomas Merton, "The Inner Experience," chap. 8.

8. John of the Cross, *The Dark Night,* book 1, chap. 1.

9. Louis Lallemant, S.J., *Spiritual Doctrine* prin. VII, chap. 4, art. 4, as cited by Reginald Garrigou-LaGrange in *The Three Ages of the Spiritual Life* vol. 2 (New York: Herder and Herder, 1948), chap. 1. Lallemant was a mystical theologian and spiritual writer of the seventeenth century who affirmed that contemplation was necessary to nourish apostolic activity and to enable us to discern the delicate movements of the Holy Spirit in our heart to guide us in all of life's events and situations.

5. The Testimony of Jung

1. Carl Jung, *Collected Works,* vol. 1, *Letters,* ed. H. Read, Bollinger Series (Princeton: Princeton University Press, 1974), 387.

2. Carl Jung, *Psychology and Alchemy,* as quoted by R. Hostie,

Religion and the Psychology of Jung (New York: Sheed and Ward, 1957), 171.

3. Carl Jung, *Collected Works,* vol. 10, ed. H. Read Bollinger Series (Princeton: Princeton University Press, 1974), par. 509.

4. Christopher Bryant, *Jung and the Christian Way* (San Francisco: Harper and Row, 1983), 48.

5. Jung, *Collected Works,* vol. 10, par. 493.

6. Jung, *Letters,* 1:387.

6. Many Are Called

1. Thomas Merton, private audio tape, unpublished.

2. Reginald Garrigou-LaGrange, *Christian Perfection and Contemplation* (New York: Herder and Herder, 1937), 163.

7. Few Are Chosen

1. Francis de Sales, *On the Love of God,* book 8, (Rockford, Ill.: Tan Books, 1974), 63.

2. Teresa of Avila, *The Way of Perfection,* chap. 20.

3. Reginald Garrigou-LaGrange, *Christian Perfection and Contemplation* (New York: Herder and Herder, 1937), 91.

4. Teresa of Avila, *The Interior Castle,* fifth mansion, chap. 1.

5. LaGrange, *Christian Perfection and Contemplation,* 378.

6. Ibid.

7. Teresa of Avila, *The Way of Perfection,* chap. 20, art. 3.

8. Beyond Church

1. For a more complete commentary on "The Book of Degrees," see Abbot André Louf, O.C.S.O., *The Work of God: A Way of Prayer,* Cistercian Studies 24 (Trappist, Ky.: Abbey of Gethsemani, 1991), 64–71.

2. George A. Maloney, S.J., *Bright Darkness* (Denville, N.J.: Dimension Books, 1977), 10–11.

9. Called into God's Own Life

1. George A. Maloney, *To Be Filled with the Fullness of God* (New Rochelle, N.Y.: New City Press, 1973), 73.

2. Thomas Merton, *The Ascent to Truth* (New York: Viking Press, 1959), 313.

3. Maloney, *To Be Filled with the Fullness of God,* 9.

4. Karl Rahner, *The Trinity* (New York: Herder & Herder, 1969), 10–11.

5. Thomas Merton, informal talk given at a prayer conference in Calcutta, October 1968, published in *The Asian Journal* (New York: New Directions, 1973), 308.

6. Thomas Merton, *Life and Holiness* (New York: Herder & Herder, 1963), 4.

10. The Primacy of Prayer

1. Thomas Merton, private audio tape, unpublished.

2. St. John Climacus, "On Prayer," *The Ladder of Divine Ascent,* Classics of Western Spirituality (Rahway, N.J.: Paulist Press, 1982), 275.

3. Reginald Garrigou-LaGrange, *Christian Perfection and Contemplation* (New York: Herder and Herder, 1937), 209.

4. Thomas Merton, quoted in *Thomas Merton — Preview of the Asian Journey,* ed. Walter Capps (New York: Crossroad, 1989), 51.

5. As cited in A. Durand, trans., *St. Chantal on Prayer* (Boston: Daughters of St. Paul Press, 1967), back cover.

6. St. Isaac the Syrian (seventh century), *Daily Readings with St. Isaac the Syrian* (Springfield, Ill.: Templegate Publishers, 1989), 75.

7. Teresa of Avila, *The Way of Perfection,* chap. 21, art. 6.

11. A Time, a Place Apart

1. Thomas Merton, *New Seeds of Contemplation* (New York: New Directions, 1961), 81.

12. The Monkey Mind

1. It is worth noting Teresa's observation that even in the so-called Prayer of Quiet — a very high state of prayer — the lower faculties still intrude. She writes: "In this state, however the understanding, memory and imagination are not captivated by divine action. Often during this prayer you will not know what to do with your understanding and memory, which will never cease to be agitated" (*Way of Perfection,* chap. 31).

2. Thomas Philippe, O.P., *The Contemplative Life* (New York: Crossroad, 1990), 37–38.

3. Thomas Merton, *New Seeds of Contemplation* (Staten Island, N.Y.: New Directions, 1961), 235.

4. A. Durand, trans., *St. Chantal on Prayer* (Boston: Daughters of St. Paul, 1968), 32.

5. George A. Maloney, S.J., *Inward Stillness* (Denville, N.J.: New Dimensions, 1976), 17.

13. Pure Prayer

1. Evagrius Ponticus, *Chapters on Prayer*, trans. Dom Eudes Bamberger, O.C.S.O., Cistercian Studies, 1970, 74–75. Evagrius was an Egyptian Desert Father (d. 399), spiritual father of John Cassian, and one of the great early teachers of the Church. His major works have been discovered only recently in this century.

2. *The Cloud of Unknowing* (anonymous), a fourteenth-century spiritual classic (Classics of Western Spirituality [Rahway, N.J.: Paulist Press, 1981], 130).

14. Silence Whole and Healing

1. It would be interesting to draw parallels between the Christian contemplative experience of God in silence (and *as* Silence) and the Buddhist concept of Shunyata, or Emptiness. Contemplation is experienced only in silence, and therefore it can be said that it is an *experience of silence*, and also of *emptiness*. For the Christian this silence is grounded in Love and is, paradoxically, a fullness — in ineffable fecundity most delicate and most real. The Buddhist might describe the experience of emptiness as the awakening of his or her Buddha nature. The Buddhist assures us that this discovery in emptiness is also, paradoxically, an experience of fullness. Here is an example of the difficulty faced in Christian-Buddhist dialogue: a word like "emptiness," which means different things to Christian and Buddhist, and the difficulty in attempting to make them coincide.

2. Max Picard, *The World of Silence* (Chicago: Henry Regnery Co., 1952), 22. Max Picard was a Swiss diagnostician at the University of Heidelberg until, becoming disillusioned with the mechanical aspect of medicine, gave up his practice to study philosophy. The son of Jewish parents, he converted to Catholicism in 1939. His writings became influential among European thinkers and philosophers, including the great Catholic philosopher Garbriel Marcel.

3. St. Isaac of Syria, *Daily Readings with St. Isaac of Syria* (Springfield, Ill.: Templegate Publishers, 1989), 46. St. Isaac, sometimes called Isaac of Nineveh, was one of the greatest spiritual writers of the East (seventh century) and is greatly regarded by the Eastern Church.

4. Picard, *The World of Silence*, 18–19.

5. Thomas Philippe, O.P., *The Contemplative Life* (New York: Crossroad, 1990), 37–38. Thomas Philippe is founder of L'Eay Vive, international center for the pursuit of wisdom seeking to integrate philosophy, theology and the spiritual life. Since 1964 he has been chaplain of L'Arche, founded by Jean Vanier, now an international ministry to the handicapped and maladjusted. He previously taught philosophy and theology at the Angelicum in Rome for many years until sickness and deafness forced him to give up teaching.

6. For an insightful commentary of this aspect of Jungian psychology see Robert A. Johnson, *Owning Your Own Shadow: Understanding the Dark Side of the Psyche* (San Francisco: Harper and Row, 1991).

7. Karl Rahner, *Theological Investigations,* vol. 9 (New York: Seabury, 1979), 118.

8. Thomas Merton, *New Seeds of Contemplation* (New York: New Directions, 1961), 235.

9. Thomas Merton, *Contemplative Prayer* (New York: Herder and Herder, 1969), 12–13. Abbé Monchanin was a French Benedictine who founded an ashram in Southern India and devoted his life to prayer, meditation, and absorbing the culture and spiritual traditions of India. He was followed by another French Benedictine, Henri Le Saux (Abhishiktananda) and still later, in Tamil Nadu, by the English Benedictine Bede Griffiths, who died in 1993 at the age of eighty-six.

15. The Hour of Silent Offering

1. William Johnson, S.J., *Being in Love* (London: Fount Paperbacks, 1988), 47.

2. Swami Muktananda was head of the Siddha Lineage of Hinduism until he died in 1981. The Siddha mantra, *Om Namah Shivaya* ("I honor the Divine within" is considered — as are all sacred mantras — as *chaitanya*, or alive, with the power to awaken the inner meditative energy called *kundalini*. It is taught that once this potential is awakened, silent meditation occurs spontaneously and spiritual evolution accelerates naturally. This conforms closely with the teachings on the Jesus Prayer whereby in time this prayer, upon entering the heart, "prays itself" under the inspiration of the Holy Spirit, engendering a habitual awareness of the presence of God.

3. John Cassian, *Conferences on Prayer,* Classics of Western Spirituality (Rahway, N.J.: Paulist Press, 1985), 131.

4. Daniel J. O'Hanlon S.J., *The Influence of Eastern Traditions on Thomas Merton's Personal Prayer,* Cistercian Studies 26 (Spencer, Mass.: St. Joseph's Abbey, 1991–92).

5. Thomas Keating, O.C.S.O., as cited in his privately distributed "Vision Statement to Contemplative Outreach," 1993.

6. Ibid.

7. George A. Maloney, "Inscape," privately distributed, December 1993.

8. See our chapter 25, "Prayer Paths to Contemplation."

16. The Garden of the Night

1. John Cassian, *Conferences on Prayer,* Classics of Western Spirituality Series (Rahway, N.J.: Paulist Press, 1985), 126–27.

2. John of the Cross, *The Dark Night,* book 1, chap. 8, art. 3.

3. Thomas Merton, *New Seeds of Contemplation* (New York: New Directions, 1961), 221.

17. As Prometheus Chained

1. Pseudo-Dionysius, *The Divine Names,* Classics of Western Spirituality, (Mahwah, N.J.: Paulist Press, 1985), chap. 1, par. 2. Until recently, it was assumed that this writer was Dionysius the Aereopagite, a convert of St. Paul (Acts 17:34). His writings thereby took on a sub-apostolic authority and had great influence on the spirituality of the Middle Ages. It remained for modern scholarship and research to determine that these were the writings of a sixth-century Syrian mystic. His treatise "The Mystical Theology," while brief, was the basis for Western apophatic theology and writings down through the centuries. "Apophatic" refers to the "dark or negative way" to God, which John of the Cross commented upon so profoundly.

2. The Eastern Church does not have a doctrine of purgatory, believing there are inadequate scriptural references to posit such a concept. However, Orthodoxy believes in hell (a state, not a "place") and teaches that our prayers and good works can liberate many who are in this alienated state of being. So teaches St. Gregory of Nyssa and other Easter Fathers.

18. God Said: Let There Be Darkness

1. Thomas Merton, *New Seeds of Contemplation* (New York: New Directions, 1961), 235.

2. John of the Cross, *The Dark Night,* book 1, chap. 3, art. 3.

3. Ibid.

4. Ibid., chap. 8, art. 3.

5. Merton, "The Inner Experience," chap. 12.
6. Merton, *New Seeds of Contemplation,* 239.

19. Embrace the Night

1. John of the Cross, *The Dark Night,* book 1, chap. 9 art. 6.
2. John of the Cross, *Ascent of Mt. Carmel,* book 2, chap. 24.
3. Ibid., book 2, chap. 4.
4. Ibid., book 2, chap. 9.
5. Teresa of Avila, *The Way of Perfection,* chap. 25.

20. Gifts of the Night

1. John of the Cross, *The Dark Night,* book 1, chap. 13, par. 3.
2. Ibid., chap. 12, art. 7.
3. Thomas Merton, *Contemplative Prayer* (New York: Herder and Herder, 1969), 96.
4. Dogmatic Constitution on the Church (*Lumen Gentium*), art. 41.
5. John of the Cross, *The Dark Night,* chap. 13, art. 4.

21. That Your Joy May Be Full

1. Thomas Merton, *Conjectures of a Guilty Bystander* (New York: Doubleday, 1966), 152.
2. Merton, "The Inner Experience," chap. 8.
3. Karl Rahner, "Mysticism, Nature and History," *Encyclopedia of Theology* (New York: Seabury Press, 1975).
4. John of the Cross, *The Dark Night,* book 1, chap. 2, art. 2.
5. Ibid., chap. 2, art. 5.
6. John of the Cross, *The Ascent of Mt. Carmel,* book 2, chap. 4, art. 2.
7. John of the Cross, *The Dark Night,* book 2, chap. 1, art. 1.
8. Teresa of Avila, *The Interior Castle,* fifth mansion, chap. 1.
9. Letter of a Carmelite prioress to Reginald LaGrange, cited in *Christian Perfection and Contemplation* (New York: Herder and Herder, 1937), 165, n. 17.
10. John of the Cross, *Ascent of Mt. Carmel,* book 2, chap. 13.
11. Pierre Teilhard de Chardin, *Hymn of the Universe* (New York: Harper & Row, 1961), Pensées 154.

22. Presence Is Prayer

1. George A. Maloney, S.J., preface, *Pseudo Macarius*, Classics of Western Spirituality (Rahway, N.J.: Paulist Press, 1992), xvi.

2. *Pseudo Macarius*, "Homily 15," 116.

3. Vladimir Lossky, *The Mystical Theology of the Eastern Church* (Crestwood, N.Y.: St. Vladimir Press, 1976), 208. Vladimir Lossky, a layman, was one of the great Eastern Orthodox theologians of the twentieth century.

23. The Signs We Are Called

1. All John of the Cross quotes are from *The Dark Night*, book 1, chap. 9. Chap. 10 of this volume deals with how we should conduct ourselves during this purifying passage and is recommended reading.

2. Thomas Merton, "The Inner Experience," chap. 5.

3. John of the Cross teaches that discursive meditation is intermittently possible for some who are not strong enough to be continually deprived of sense satisfaction, at least at the outset of the Dark Night.

4. Reginald Garrigou-LaGrange, *The Three Ages of the Spiritual Life* (New York Herder and Herder, 1948), 2:50.

24. Spiritual Direction

1. John of the Cross, *The Dark Night*, book 1, chap. 11, art. 2.

2. Ibid., book 2, chap. 10, art. 2.

3. Juan Gonzales Arintero, O.P., *The Mystical Evolution in the Development and Vitality of the Church* (New York: Herder and Herder, 1951), 2:80–81.

4. George A. Maloney, S.J., *Journey into Contemplation* (New York: Living Flame Press, 1983), 92.

5. Thomas Merton, *Spiritual Direction and Meditation* (Collegeville, Minn.: Liturgical Press, 1960), chap. 4.

6. John of the Cross, *The Living Flame of Love*, chap. 3, art. 30–31.

26. The Long Journey Home

1. As cited by Reginald Garrigou-LaGrange, *Christian Perfection and Contemplation* (New York: Herder and Herder, 1937), 436–37.

2. Thomas Keating, *Intimacy with God* (New York: Crossroad, 1994), 142–43.

3. Juan Gonzales Arintero, O.P., *The Mystical Evolution and the Development and Vitality of the Church* (New York: Herder & Herder, 1951), 2:105.

4. John of the Cross, *The Dark Night*, book 1, chap. 8, art. 5.

5. Reginald Garrigou-LaGrange, *Christian Perfection and Contemplation*, 190.

27. Killing Care

1. Johannes Tauler, *Second Sermon for the 20th Sunday after Trinity*, as cited in Reginald Garrigou-LaGrange, *Christian Perfection and Contemplation* (New York: Herder and Herder, 1937), 393.

2. Blaise Pascal, *Pensées* (New York: Modern Library, 1941), 47.

28. Idle Curiosity

1. *1992 National Television Index Report*, A. C. Nielsen Company. Data based on average daily family viewing hours.

29. Carnal-Minded

1. Thomas Merton, *What Is Contemplation?* (Springfield Ill.: Templegate Publishers, 1981), 7.

2. Thomas Merton, "The Inner Experience," chap. 1.

30. A Sea of Lies

1. Declaration on the Relationship of the Church to Non-Christian Religions (*Nostra Aetate*), art. 2.

2. Thomas Merton, "The Inner Experience," chap. 1.

3. Karl Rahner, *On Prayer* (New York: Paulist Press, 1958), 52.

31. Contemplation and Compassion

1. Thomas Merton, "The Inner Experience," chap. 15.

2. Walter Hilton, "Letters to a Layman," trans. David L. Jeffrey in *Toward a Perfect Love* (Portland, Ore.: Multnomah Press, 1985), 19.

3. Reginald Garrigou-LaGrange, O.P., *Christian Perfection and Contemplation* (New York: Herder and Herder, 1937), 365.

4. Merton, "The Inner Experience," chap. 3.

33. Woman Who Weeps

1. Against the Nestorian heresy, which claimed that Mary was the mother only of the human Christ, the Council of Ephesus (431) declared her "Lady Theotokos." This council and the Council of Chalcedon twenty years later protected and preserved one of the essential dogmas of the Christian faith, namely, that both natures of Christ are distinct but not separated, unmixed and indivisible. The Nestorian heresy would have led to the "splitting up" of Christ into two *persons* — something even God could not manage!

2. St. Louis de Montfort, *Treatise on True Devotion to Mary* (Rockford Ill.: Tan Books, 1952).

3. Thomas Philippe, O.P., *The Fire of Contemplation* (Staten Island, N.Y.: Alba House, 1981), 112.

4. St. Louis de Montfort, *Treatise on True Devotion to Mary.*

34. Song of the Butterfly

1. Teresa of Avila, *The Way of Perfection,* chap. 21, art. 6.
2. Thomas Merton, "The Inner Experience," chap. 1.
3. John of the Cross, *The Spiritual Canticle,* chap. 29, art. 3.

Bibliography

Abhishiktananda (Henri Le Saux). *Prayer.* Philadelphia: Westminster Press, 1967.

Bolshakoff, Sergias. *Russian Mystics.* Cistercian Studies 26. Kalamazoo, Mich., 1976.

Bryant, Christopher. *Jung and the Christian Way.* San Francisco: Harper & Row, 1983.

Carter, Edward. *The Mysticism of Everyday.* New York: Sheed & Ward, 1991.

DeJaegher. *An Anthology of Christian Mysticism.* Springfield, Ill.: Templegate, 1977.

Dubay, Thomas. *The Fire Within.* San Francisco: Ignatius Press, 1989.

Enomiya-Lasalle, Hugo. *Living in the New Consciousness.* Boston: Shambhala Press, 1986.

Freeman, Laurence. *The Light Within.* New York: Crossroad, 1987.

Graham, Aelred. *Zen Catholicism.* New York: Harcourt, Brace, 1963.

———. *Contemplative Christianity.* New York: Seabury/Crossroad, 1974.

Green, Thomas. *When the Well Runs Dry.* Notre Dame, Ind.: Ave Maria Press, 1979.

———*Drinking from a Dry Well.* Notre Dame, Ind.: Ave Maria Press, 1991.

Griffiths, Bede. *Return to the Center.* Springfield, Ill., Templegate, 1976.

———. *The Golden String.* Springfield, Ill., Templegate, 1980.

———. *Marriage of East and West.* Springfield, Ill., Templegate, 1982.

———. *The Cosmic Revelation.* Springfield, Ill., Templegate, 1983.

———. *Christ in India.* Springfield, Ill., Templegate, 1984.

———. *Rivers of Compassion.* Warwick, N.Y.: Warwick, 1987.

Happold, F. C. *The Journey Inwards.* Atlanta: John Knox Press, 1968.

Higgins, John J. *Merton's Theology of Prayer.* CS 18. Kalamazoo, Mich.: Cistercian Publications, 1971.

John of the Cross. *Collected Works of St. John of the Cross.* Trans. Kieran Kavanaugh, O.C.D., and Otilio Rodriguez, O.C.D. Washington, D.C.: ICS Press. See especially *The Dark Night,* books 1 and 2, and *The Ascent of Mt. Carmel,* books 1–3.

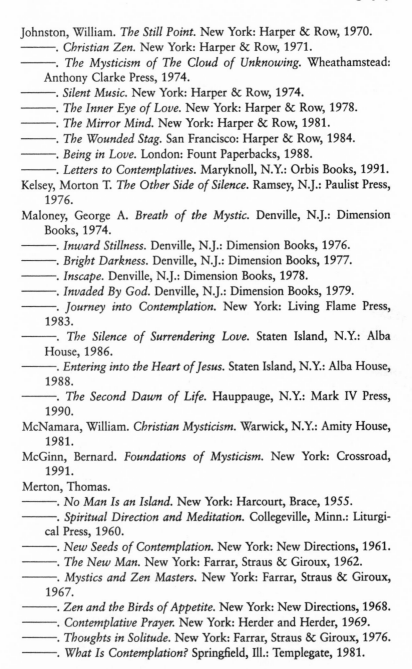

Johnston, William. *The Still Point*. New York: Harper & Row, 1970.

———. *Christian Zen*. New York: Harper & Row, 1971.

———. *The Mysticism of The Cloud of Unknowing*. Wheathamstead: Anthony Clarke Press, 1974.

———. *Silent Music*. New York: Harper & Row, 1974.

———. *The Inner Eye of Love*. New York: Harper & Row, 1978.

———. *The Mirror Mind*. New York: Harper & Row, 1981.

———. *The Wounded Stag*. San Francisco: Harper & Row, 1984.

———. *Being in Love*. London: Fount Paperbacks, 1988.

———. *Letters to Contemplatives*. Maryknoll, N.Y.: Orbis Books, 1991.

Kelsey, Morton T. *The Other Side of Silence*. Ramsey, N.J.: Paulist Press, 1976.

Maloney, George A. *Breath of the Mystic*. Denville, N.J.: Dimension Books, 1974.

———. *Inward Stillness*. Denville, N.J.: Dimension Books, 1976.

———. *Bright Darkness*. Denville, N.J.: Dimension Books, 1977.

———. *Inscape*. Denville, N.J.: Dimension Books, 1978.

———. *Invaded By God*. Denville, N.J.: Dimension Books, 1979.

———. *Journey into Contemplation*. New York: Living Flame Press, 1983.

———. *The Silence of Surrendering Love*. Staten Island, N.Y.: Alba House, 1986.

———. *Entering into the Heart of Jesus*. Staten Island, N.Y.: Alba House, 1988.

———. *The Second Dawn of Life*. Hauppauge, N.Y.: Mark IV Press, 1990.

McNamara, William. *Christian Mysticism*. Warwick, N.Y.: Amity House, 1981.

McGinn, Bernard. *Foundations of Mysticism*. New York: Crossroad, 1991.

Merton, Thomas.

———. *No Man Is an Island*. New York: Harcourt, Brace, 1955.

———. *Spiritual Direction and Meditation*. Collegeville, Minn.: Liturgical Press, 1960.

———. *New Seeds of Contemplation*. New York: New Directions, 1961.

———. *The New Man*. New York: Farrar, Straus & Giroux, 1962.

———. *Mystics and Zen Masters*. New York: Farrar, Straus & Giroux, 1967.

———. *Zen and the Birds of Appetite*. New York: New Directions, 1968.

———. *Contemplative Prayer*. New York: Herder and Herder, 1969.

———. *Thoughts in Solitude*. New York: Farrar, Straus & Giroux, 1976.

———. *What Is Contemplation?* Springfield, Ill.: Templegate, 1981.

————. *Conjectures of a Guilty Bystander*. New York: Image Books, 1989.

Moore, Robert L. *Carl Jung and Christian Spirituality*. Mahwah, N.J.: Paulist Press, 1988.

Philippe, Thomas. *The Fire of Contemplation*. Staten Island, N.Y.: Alba House, 1981.

————. *The Contemplative Life*. New York: Crossroad, 1990.

Rahner, Karl. *On Prayer*. Mahwah, N.J.: Paulist Press, 1958.

————. *Encounters with Silence*. New York: Newman Press, 1960.

————. *A Rahner Reader*. Ed. Gerald McCool. New York: Crossroad/ Seabury, 1975.

————. *The Content of Faith*. New York: Crossroad, 1992.

————. *Foundations of Christian Faith*. New York: Crossroad, 1993.

Raguin, Yves. *Paths to Contemplation*. Wheathamstead, Eng.: Anthony Clarke, 1975.

Sanford, John A. *Mystical Christianity*. New York: Crossroad, 1994.

Steindl-Rast, David. *Gratefulness at the Heart of Prayer*. Mahwah, N.J.: Paulist Press, 1984.

————. *A Listening Heart*. New York: Crossroad, 1987.

Teresa of Avila. *Collected Works of Teresa of Avila*. Trans. Kieran Kavanaugh, O.C.D., and Otilio Rodriguez, O.C.D. Washington, D.C.: ICS Press. See especially *The Interior Castle, The Way of Perfection,* and *The Book of Her Life*.

Tilman, Klemens. *The Practice of Meditation*. Mahwah, N.J.: Paulist Press, 1977.

Underhill, Evelyn. *Practical Mysticism*. New York: E. P. Dutton, 1943.

————. *Mysticism*. New York: E. P. Dutton, 1961.

Voillaume, René. *The Need for Contemplation*. Denville, N.J.: Dimension Books, 1972.

————. *Spirituality from the Desert*. Huntington, Ind.: Our Sunday Visitor, 1975.

Writings on the Four Christian Prayer Paths Cited in Chapter 25

On Centering Prayer

Keating, Thomas. *Open Heart, Open Mind*. Rockford, Mass.: Element, 1986.

————. *Invitation to Love*. Rockford, Mass.: Element, 1992.

————. *Intimacy with God*. New York: Crossroad, 1994.

Pennington, Basil. *Centering Prayer*. New York: Image Books, 1982.

————. *Centered Living*. New York: Image Books, 1988.

On the Jesus Prayer

Maloney, George A. *Prayer of the Heart*. Notre Dame, Ind.: Ave Maria Press, 1981.
———. *Centering on the Lord Jesus*. Everette, Wash.: Performance Press, 1982.
Brianchaninov, Bishop. *On the Prayer of Jesus*. London: John Watkins, 1965.
Kadloubovsky, E. *Writings from the Philokalia on Prayer of the Heart*. London: Faber & Faber, 1973.

On the Christian Mantra

Main, John. *Word into Silence*. Mahwah, N.J.: Paulist Press, 1981.
———. *The Way of Unknowing*. New York: Crossroad, 1990.

On the Rosary

Pennington, Basil. *Praying by Hand*. New York: Doubleday.
Keating, Thomas. *Intimacy with God*. New York: Crossroad, 1994.

On *Lectio Divina*

Keating, Thomas. *Intimacy with God*. New York: Crossroad, 1994.
Hall, Thelma. *Too Deep for Words*. Mahwah, N.J.: Paulist Press, 1988.